The GOD Chair

One Thousand Days of Pain with Purpose

ANN BECKHAM GAINEY

WESTBOW
P R E S S®
A DIVISION OF THOMAS NELSON
& ZONDERVAN

This book is a work of non-fiction. Unless otherwise noted, the author and the publisher make no explicit guarantees as to the accuracy of the information contained in this book and in some cases, names of people and places have been altered to protect their privacy.

WestBow Press books may be ordered through booksellers or by contacting:

WestBow Press
A Division of Thomas Nelson & Zondervan
1663 Liberty Drive
Bloomington, IN 47403
www.westbowpress.com
1 (866) 928-1240

Interior pictures–Elliott Gainey and Jessica Chambers
Author Image–OldEdwardsinn.com

ISBN: 978-1-9736-7527-3 (sc)
ISBN: 978-1-9736-7528-0 (hc)
ISBN: 978-1-9736-7526-6 (e)

Library of Congress Control Number: 2019915242

Printed in the United States of America.

WestBow Press rev. date: 12/11/2019

CONTENTS

THE TRIGGER

THE TENSION

THE TRIBULATION

THE TRIP

THE TASK

THE TRIUMPH

Jentezen Franklin-

The God chair---everyone has sat in it, and many are sitting in it right now. Ann's personal experience with pain has qualified her to speak with authority on this topic. Her heart for hurting people adds an extraordinary grace that will touch your heart and give you hope.

—**Jentezen Franklin**, *New York Times*
bestselling author and pastor

Cal Thomas-

When I first met Ann Gainey I was so impressed by her energy that I nicknamed her "fireball Ann." That energy, along with the Lord's healing, has given her a new purpose in life: to minister to many others confronted with physical and other challenges. You, or someone you know, will be blessed and encouraged by her testimony.

—**Cal Thomas,** Syndicated Columnist

With gratitude and deep love

For my husband whom I have loved since our eyes
locked when we were sixteen. For years, you have
encouraged me to write a book. Well, Al, here it is.

And for our wonderful children, Mary Katherine
and Elliott. You made our house a home.

And for God, the Great Planner of our lives, by whom we are blessed.

**To my godly parents, Mary Emma Hendrix
Beckham and Roy Elliott Bynum Beckham**

They taught me, at an early age, to love the Lord with all my heart, soul, mind, and strength, and to love my neighbor as myself.

They complimented my strengths, but I wasn't demeaned for my weaknesses.

They loved me as God created me to be.

As a child and then as an adult, I watched my parents love people and show them "Jesus with skin on."

Mama's homegoing was October 2008 at the age of eighty. Alzheimer's teaches families a great deal about the wedding vows "in sickness and in health, until death do us part." For ten years, Daddy made those words personal, as his children and adult grandchildren watched that God-message play out before our eyes.

At this writing, Daddy is ninety-two and still serving the Lord each day. God has provided him a mission field right at his doorstep. He is missing no opportunities, and God is smiling.

Thank You, Lord, for placing me in Mary and Roy's arms and home … better known as Mama and Daddy.

Daddy says quite often that God is good in His greatness and great in His goodness. You are so right, Daddy. Preach on.

IN APPRECIATION

"I don't know how to write a book." Friends were kindly encouraging me, but I felt out of my comfort zone. After I said those exact words to fifteen ladies over fifteen lunches, I thought that God would take no for an answer. I knew better than that. He rarely does, and He didn't this time either. But He did bring these people, unbeknownst to me, without my seeking them out, several of whom I didn't know. Sounds just like Him, huh?

As He brought them to me, one at a miraculous time, He smiled and lovingly said to my anxious heart, "Now what's your excuse, Ann?" I had none.

First it was Beth Wilson. Next, Madeline Wirt. Followed by Lillian Welch. Then Candi Long and Ramona Elrod came aboard. Debbie Thomas asked if I knew Lynda Young. I didn't but called her. Soon after that, Sylvia Pifer offered her time. Then Debra Folsom and Emily McCoy joined the happy throng.

It became a domino effect, and each woman offered a different expertise. How could I turn them down? I would have been turning God down.

"Ann, do you think that what I taught you in one thousand days was just for you?" In a nervous whisper, I answered my Master. "I guess not, Sir." With timid trepidation, I humbly stepped out by faith, putting pen to paper.

So this is God's book. He is the lead character, receiving top billing. I have a mere bit part to play. I believe He chose me for this health journey and for the task of writing this story down.

These words are for your soul, just as they were for mine as I lived them each day. Why? Because He loves you and me that much.

Obey Him with glad reckless joy.
—Oswald Chambers

FOREWORD

Martha Beckham Morgan

On June 17, 2017, my sister, Ann, texted me, "If I have to live the way I feel today for twenty-five more years, I'd rather go see Mama now." Our Mama had been in heaven for nine years at the time.

Flashback to the 1950s: Picture a young minister, his wife, and their three children: Ann, the firstborn, Earl, the boy, and Martha, the baby. I, Martha, am hiding behind Mama's skirt-tail, Earl is the one in his Sunday suit, and Ann is posing both of us for the picture.

I consider Ann a natural-born leader, as she takes responsibility very seriously; she's goal-oriented and an organizer. She is also very personable, creative, and talented. Earl and I remember her directing us in little Christmas plays for Mama and Daddy, complete with homemade programs of construction paper and Crayolas.

I think of Ann as a natural-born helper. She is concerned about every individual's well-being, from the womb to the tomb. After graduating from college with a BA in elementary education, she devoted herself to her students. The children thrived on her energy and antics.

Later in life, Ann devoted twenty-five years to unborn children and their parents, as executive director of Choices Pregnancy Care Center in Gainesville, Georgia. She affected many lives through her career and continues to influence many more. She identifies her help to others as a ministry. In her retirement, she senses her call is to minister to others as a burden bearer.

Ann has always been there for me: when my twenty-six-year-old husband was diagnosed with chronic myelogenous leukemia; when he and I, despite his illness, wanted to adopt a child; and when he died at age thirty-two, not long after the adoption process began. She was by my side at the funeral home when, during my time of despair, the funeral staff instructed me to pick out a casket and a vault. What does a young widow know about vaults? I remember Ann whispering, "We should be picking out a cradle or a crib, not a casket and a vault."

Ann was there after I remarried and when I was going through infertility treatments in my late thirties. She rejoiced when I had my son but cried with me as the marriage became difficult and ended in divorce. She has always been my burden bearer. I was unprepared to be hers, especially over the 215 miles between us.

As preacher's kids, we learned that God loves us and uses our struggles to draw us to Him. In His hands, He is the Potter, and we are the clay. Being the clay is painful, but God desires each of us to become the work of art He sculpted long before the world He created fell into sin. I know it perfectly in my head, but this is my big sister, my role model, my encourager, and my burden bearer, and on receiving the text about how she'd rather go see Mama now, I was scared.

Thankfully, I was able to take time off work to spend several days with Ann. The longer I was around her, though, the more alarmed I became about her physical and emotional state. I realized she had been trying to protect us by putting on a good show, rather than letting us know just how serious her condition had become.

Ann and I remained in constant contact over the next months. She went through arduous trips to multiple specialists and endured numerous tests; unfortunately, the results offered up no diagnosis or even some kind of treatment to help in the meantime. I was being the burden bearer my sister had been for me.

During our conversations, Ann began sharing how she was able to minister to people God seemed to be putting along her path. I was excited that God was using her, a natural-born helper, in a mission field again. My hope was that one day, God could use her again as a natural-born leader as well. How, though? She was so weak and having to undergo so much. In addition, there was still the occasional text referring to Mama in heaven.

But God, in His mercy and goodness, provided the doctors with the diagnosis. There remained a long recovery process, but God has healed our precious Ann. As she began to open up and share her story, I, along with many others, said, "You should write a book." As you read Ann's words, she will take you through her journey, not to display herself, but to highlight her Lord. She realizes your struggle will be different from hers, but she desires to be your burden bearer. More importantly, she yearns to lead you to her Lord, the Great Physician and Ultimate Burden Bearer. God created you, loves you, and wants to be the one you turn to during your hour of need and during each moment of every day.

"MY STORY"

Big Daddy Weave
Songwriters: Mike Weaver and Jason Ingram

If I told you my story
You would hear Hope that wouldn't let go
You would hear Love that never gave up
You would hear Life, but it wasn't mine.
This is my story, this is my song.
Praising my Savior all the day long.
Oh to tell you my story is to tell of Him.

Ann's story

S Severely
T tested
O over time, then
R restored for
Y Your purposes.

THE TRIGGER

CHAPTER 1

The Assignment

Then Samuel [and Ann] said, "Speak, for your servant is listening."
—1 Samuel 3:10 (NIV)

"This is your homework, Ann," my new counselor said as I got out my pen to write in the fresh notebook. "We humans are very good at *doing* but not as good at *being*. It is the fast-paced world in which we live, isn't it? Therefore, for your homework this week, I want you to find a place to be with God each day. Now here are the rules."

Rules? I thought. *I've always been a very orderly, conscientious person. I'm great at abiding by guidelines.* I sat up straight, almost at rapt attention, and prepared my pen to write as she spoke.

"You are not to have an open Bible with you," Elizabeth continued. "You may not have a devotional book. No Bible study. No items. Just you and God with no agenda."

She paused for a moment as if to study my body language, observing how I was receiving her instructions. I kept my head down and scribbled rapidly, hoping she wouldn't see the myriad of questions and thoughts circling through my head. I couldn't recall ever sitting before the Lord for any length of time without a well-laid-out plan. Nevertheless, I was determined to make an A on this assignment—no matter what.

"Ann, sit with the Lord. Just you and Him. And let me repeat: no agenda."

I closed my notebook slowly, looked up, and attempted a smile through my confusion. "Got it," I replied, taking in as deep a breath as I could muster. *After all,* I thought as I prepared to leave, *I'm a people pleaser who wants to do things right. This sounds simple enough.*

For my time with God, I determined to find a special place. It had to be a very special place. I chose the stately, blue wing-backed chair in our living room, mainly because there was a window nearby. It somehow seemed appropriate to look at the sky when I talked with God. In addition, I liked the tall trees around the deck. They would be my wall of protection so that I wouldn't see the road with the cars and people passing by. No distractions. This would be fun.

Next, I gathered my soft, well-worn slippers and placed them under the chair. It needed to look a bit cozier. Yes, the slippers did help. Then I thought of the burgundy throw blanket. It was delightfully soft, like a heavenly cloud, and even had pockets for when I might get chilly and could wrap myself up. *This is coming together rather nicely*, I thought with pride, pushing my shoulders back in agreement. I draped the shawl across the corner and along the arm of the chair, stepping back to admire. *Yes, the chair is very inviting. I'm ready.*

No, not quite. It still needs to look a bit more reverent. Ah, yes. The cross.

I hurried into our bedroom to retrieve the artwork that meant so much to me. It was a heavy cross constructed out of nails with "Amazing Grace" written in the middle. Over a foot tall, it made a profound statement. I placed it on the hearth near the chair, attempting to stand it up between the wall and the fireplace. That would be the best place for viewing. Unfortunately, it didn't appear secure as the cross was heavy, so after some mental discussion, I decided to lay it flat on the hearth. Stepping back, I crossed my arms and then smiled with satisfaction and a little glee. *Now I'm ready for my God time.*

I enjoy projects. This was like a to-do list for me, proudly checking each item off in my mind.

Yet I still couldn't sit in the chair. Why? I walked by it several times a day. It drew me, but I avoided getting close. I stared at the chair, and it seemed to stare back at me. This wasn't as simple as I had thought.

The following week at my next session, I managed a half-smile toward Elizabeth. "Well, I finished half of my homework," I said. I wondered if a little humor would get me off the hook.

I even showed her the picture on my phone as proof. *Didn't that part count?* I rationalized silently. However, I knew that I couldn't show up for the next week's appointment without completing the rest of her assignment.

People pleasers wouldn't do that, and I was one.

Therefore, the next day, after unloading the groceries, I said, in a command of sorts, "After lunch, I *will* sit in that chair." I was determined but anxious.

As I ate my sandwich, I looked at the chair, taking longer than usual to eat. It was evident that I was stalling. This was a conflict. The arms of the chair were in a tug-of-war with me because of my overthinking temperament. I felt lovingly invited by the God of the universe to rest with Him, yet I wanted to do it perfectly. Perhaps I would be disappointed in my efforts. Who would win this struggle?

Questions swirled through my mind:

What do I say to God?

Will I hear if He says something to me?

How long do I sit?

When will I know that it's time to get up?

Do I need to leave Al's supper on a plate?

I had so many other pressing things on tap each day. Just the thought of adding anything else to my list while trying to keep all the other plates twirling in the air made it harder than usual to breathe. And physical therapy (PT) three times a week was exhausting. Yet I knew that all of this procrastination was nothing more than the deceiver of my mind attacking my Achilles' heel of weariness. I wasn't going to let him win this battle, so I would press on, regardless.

People pleasers wouldn't quit. Frustrated, I prayed, "Lord, I know Elizabeth told me not to have anything to read. But Sir, if You say something to me that I really don't want to forget, may I have a notepad and pen to write it down? I won't keep it on my lap. It will be on the floor a yard away. I promise."

I immediately felt a peace flood over me and knew that the Master of my heart was giving me His permission. *What a relief. Now I'm finally ready. I can do this.*

With the small pad and pen a distance away on the wood floor, I tentatively sat down, wondering if I would survive this seemingly herculean task. "Lord, I'm confident that You know my deep love for You, so You are aware that my deep desire is to sit at Your feet. But at the same time, I don't know how to do it."

I sensed Him gently whisper in my ear, "That's the point, Ann. Don't do anything. Just be with Me."

Ah, permission to be. My body began to relax. He wasn't looking for a performance. He just wanted to be with me. Perhaps knowing that would make me calmly confident.

I cautiously sat in the chair, looking up toward the sky. White clouds on a blue landscape. Trees waving on His heavenly canvas. Had I ever studied, really looked at, the vastness of creation this long? At one time?

For about fifteen minutes, I heard nothing. All was quiet, yet all was well with my soul. My heart felt safe.

I was resting in Him and with Him. It was evident.

But sitting here this quietly caused me to notice my shallow breathing more than usual, and I was trying to forget the physical issues I was dealing with. I felt despondent. But sadness and tension weren't what I needed right now. I managed to say weakly, yet bravely, from the depths of my soul, "Lord, I want Your breath in me. I need a second wind."

It was at that moment that God began to talk to me.

God: Ann, you may not feel evergreen like these trees off the deck. But my desire for you is to feel evergreen, the way I created you to be. You are my Evergreen Ann. I didn't create human *doings*. I created human *beings*. Remember that often.

Me: Lord, I want more of You.

God: Ann, why would you want more of Me when you could have *all* of Me?

Me: Lord, how do I get *all* of You?

God: By sitting at My feet like you are. I have great work for you, but no greater work than for My Ann to bask in My presence.

Me: Lord, I want *all* of Your tears as well. I've held my tears inside for so long, and I'm bone-tired. And Lord, thank You for allowing the sun to shine for a moment on this somewhat cloudy day. I'm reminded of the old 1960s song by the 5th Dimension: "Let the Sunshine In."

God: Ann, let the Son shine into your entire being, for I warm you better than the sun ever could.

After forty-five minutes, I felt His gentle nod that we were finished for a time. As I was getting up to leave, I tilted my head to heaven and said with a smile, "This is my God chair."

Explanation

Just for the record, I have never heard the audible voice of God. Yet when I sit before Him, wait upon Him, and listen intently to Him in my God chair, He reveals deep things for me to learn. I grow closer to Him, and I grow in my walk with Him the more I avail myself of Him and His infinite wisdom.

As you read the journal entries at the end of each chapter, you will notice that they are not in chronological order. I believe that God led me to a specific entry that fit the topic of each chapter. He's like that.

We never know when what we hear from God will be relevant, meaningful, and timely for a specific life situation at a different time, do we?

The journal began long before I received the God-nudge to write this book, proving, once again, that He is the Best Planner ever. He is awesome and ever amazing to me.

To God be the glory, great things He has done.

CHAPTER 2

The Injury

(Told by my husband, Al)

This explains why a man leaves his father and mother and
is joined to his wife, and the two are united into one.
—Genesis 2:24 (NLT)

It started as a normal day. Up at 5 a.m., quiet time, treadmill, shower, dress, prayer with Ann, a goodbye kiss, and a cup of coffee before leaving the house for the office. Ann drove one mile to work at Choices Pregnancy Care Center in Gainesville, Georgia, where she has ministered to pregnant women over the past twenty-five years. Yes, it started as a typical day. Little were we to know what was on the horizon.

It was a particularly long day. As I arrived home after six o'clock, Ann came out of our bedroom and appeared panicked. "I can hardly breathe!" she exclaimed.

Her shoulders were rising and falling in short, rapid successions. The pupils of her eyes were pinpoints, as if oxygen deprived. Concern and fear gripped me, as this wasn't like the Ann I had known for nearly fifty years. I held her briefly to provide some comfort, noticing that she was gasping for air.

"We need to go to the emergency room immediately," I said, attempting to remain calm for her sake. My first thought was that she was having a heart attack or perhaps had a blood clot in her lung.

She thought I was overreacting and said in her "Ann" way, "Just let me go to bed. I'll be fine in the morning."

With labored breath, Ann informed me of what had happened. She had worked all day and then gone late that afternoon for a simple medical procedure. She was breathing well upon arrival to her appointment but came away unable to breathe in a normal rhythm.

This normal day was the beginning of a two-and-one-half-year trial and error in search for answers. Doctor after doctor, test after test, locally in Gainesville and forty miles away in Atlanta, with no diagnosis. Neurosurgeons, cardiologists, neurologists, pulmonologists, neuromuscular specialists, and ENTs were involved; they all wanted to discover the cause. Every doctor had yet another test to perform. But every test came back negative.

This was incredibly frustrating for me as a husband who, more than anything, wanted to fix this problem for my wife. I couldn't imagine how Ann was feeling, both physically and emotionally. Had it not been for her strong relationship with God and her incredible will to plow through each day, I'm not sure where we would be today.

Ann pushed persistently during each workday, forcing herself to perform to her standards of excellence, yet when she returned home each afternoon, all she could do was collapse. She went to bed early and remained there until the next morning. Her emotional and physical state became more concerning to me with each passing day.

Nothing seemed to improve her constantly labored breathing. Even when she was sleeping, it sounded as if she was running on a treadmill.

For nearly three years, Ann went to bed worn out and woke up as exhausted as the night before. What a long time to work so hard to take every breath. It's difficult to do anything for twenty-four hours a day, seven days a week.

I'm a fix-it person. Most men are, I suppose. It became obvious that I couldn't do anything to fix it or even to improve the issue. I couldn't trade places with her, which I wanted to do, just to give her some rest. I continued to feel helpless, unable to do anything to get a genuine smile from her. She attempted to force a partial smile to allay my fears, but I knew her too well. Would this be how she had to live from now until she met the Lord?

It seemed that even my prayers were worthless. I knew better, but I was frustrated with God; no answers seemed to be found. And, believe me, we were looking everywhere. At times, I found myself angry with God. Would

I ever be able to have my wife, my best friend since we were sixteen years old, back again and have our lives return to normal?

As the days, weeks, and months passed, I became more and more anxious. Actually, I was scared about what was happening and what it might mean for us, long-term.

Daily, Ann and I were searching the internet for medical answers but only found unresolved testimonies that gave no hope. These individuals were saying that they had had similar tests, medications, procedures. Everything we read told us that nothing could help. This was the way it was and the way it was going to be. Sadly, they had reconciled that they would be unable to take a normal breath, forever.

I regularly started thinking about the past, the good times, the fun things we did together. We married at the age of twenty. Ann graduated from college early and taught elementary school while I finished my degree. We had little money, but life was simple. During the time of her illness, we began doing things we had wanted to do over the years but had postponed because my career, success, community status, and ego took precedence over caring for Ann and fostering our relationship.

I have to add an aside here for husbands: Please do not ignore your wife and children (and, I suggest, Christ as well) for things of this world. It really will take its toll later in life when you kick yourself for wasting time on stuff that really makes no difference in this life (or in eternity).

We planned vacations we had always wanted to take over the years, trips that had been on our bucket list. I thought that perhaps getting away for a while would make her feel better. We took trips with lifelong friends, so Ann would push through the pain. I knew she was miserable, but for the sake of our friends and me, she forced that Ann smile. But I knew her well. She was crying on the inside.

Her stamina, her internal fortitude, and the will to live, in my view, were fading fast. Comments like, "I don't know how much longer I can do this," were becoming more and more normal to hear each day.

I kept telling myself, "She will be better soon," but I wasn't convinced. My heart was breaking for her, for us.

Something, somebody, some answer had to be found somewhere, but what, when, how?

CHAPTER 3

Cry Me a River

> Feeling so much to be void of feeling. Crying
> tearless staring at the ceiling.
> —Jake Provance

Crying, for me, is a gentle trickle down my cheek from one eye, with a glazed touch of sadness in the other.

Any time I'm around people who know I don't cry easily, I point to the lone tear and say, "This is sobbing for me. Take a picture." Suffice it to say, I don't weep well.

Mama used the term "a crying jag." I think that means a period of uncontrolled tears. However, the only time I recall Mama crying was November 22, 1963, the day President John F. Kennedy was assassinated. It was her birthday. I always wondered if that somehow factored into her tears.

I don't recall seeing Daddy cry, either. But men typically don't show their emotions on the outside (I say "typically" because Al cries more than I do; I rest my case).

I'm not your typical female crier, sad to say. Between work and family, my plate was full, and so was my sorrow, except I had turned off my tears faucet. Every woman I knew shed tears, but not Ann.

I can be quite stoic at times, even when I should "cry me a river," as the old tune suggests. No one could catch a view of my silent tears, so my mascara and eyeliner were always in place.

Martha, my sister, can cry, and I've always been jealous of that. On my health journey, I asked if I could borrow a few of her tears. After all, isn't that what sisters do? Share? Martha wanted to do something, so she sent me a movie to watch with a note that read, "I *know* this will make you cry." It was a good story. I was touched. But moved to tears? No. I dreaded giving her that nontearful report.

It's so simple to pour a tall glass of Southern sweet tea. But tears? They didn't pour that easily for me. I could almost hear subtle sighs arise from my collapsing chest, yearning to have a crying jag. Just as quickly, though, I would feel what seemed to be a hand inside of me, pressing the tenuous tears back down. Like a vise.

I would say, "Don't do that, Ann. Let the tears flow so that the disappointments will diminish." I knew that God gives us timely tears for many reasons: tears of joy and tears of distress. Still, the tears responded to the hand, pushing my pain back down into my chest. *Lord, why do I have a tendency to suppress my tears?* I didn't have a clue. I'm sure He did, but He wasn't sharing.

During the months of seeking a diagnosis and enduring many medical tests, I only teared up once. The neuromuscular specialist had forewarned me that the next test would really hurt.

Doctors never tell you something is going to hurt, I thought. Anxiety was already building, and the appointment was a week away. I didn't want to be apprehensive that long. I went somewhere deep into myself because I didn't have time or the track record to cry.

The day finally arrived. I said nothing on the one-hour drive, but as Al pulled into a parking spot and turned off the car, I began to cry softly. He didn't know what to do. I'm sure he thought, *Ann doesn't cry. I'm not used to this. What can I say to make it better?* But he wisely said nothing.

I whispered to him, to myself, and to God, "I can't take much more of this." Scraping the bottom of the barrel for energy, I sat in silence. My thoughts and body were numb.

Since Al had turned the car off, I had no choice. It was time to go inside for the uncomfortable appointment, but he waited patiently for a signal from me.

A couple of minutes went by. "I'm ready now," I said with determination. "Let's go."

I felt like a robot. My effervescent smile exuded an air of confidence, yet my heart was frightened. Would I ever get well?

Upon entering the testing room, a large sign greeted me (I wondered why it was so huge and neon pink):

> If, at any time during this test, the pain becomes too
> severe, let the medical personnel know immediately.

Well, that certainly didn't help lower my distress. Would they notice if I ran out the door?

True to what the neuromuscular specialist had said, the test was horrific, and I had been through many painful tests in my life. But I bore it without crying. That is Ann.

The specialist gave me the results, which were negative. She had forewarned me that a positive result wouldn't be what I wanted to hear. So I had asked people to pray toward that end, yet the results felt bittersweet to my heart.

The doctor read my mind, I think, and said, "You are gratified but not satisfied."

I was grateful not to have a catastrophic illness but sadly unsatisfied with still no diagnosis.

Yep. That was it, in a nutshell. But walking out to the waiting room to face Al, I still wished I was crying. Could I cry and still be courageous?

No, Ann, I thought resolutely, *don't waste time conjuring up a tear. Time is of the essence.* What specialist was on the radar next? No time for tears, even if I was capable of crying.

The emotional pain ramped up. I tried to dial it down, but it wouldn't budge. What did I hear that was scrambling? It wasn't scrambled eggs; it was scrambled Ann.

We were both quiet on the long drive home. I was weary of appointments that ended as downers. When would I get an upper, like an easily treatable diagnosis? I recalled the old song "Big Girls Don't Cry," by the Four Seasons. As I was singing silently the words that I recalled from my teens, I remembered that the end of the song went, "big girls *do* cry."

As I looked out the window of our moving car, my eyes glazed over, but not a trickle ran down my cheek.

For crying out loud.

When will I be a big girl?

And cry.

God Chair Journal Entry

What would you have me call You when I sit in my God chair?

Call Me Sovereign Lord, Ann.

Got it, Sir.

I am the Alpha and the Omega, the Beginning and the End. Rest in that knowledge. I knew you at the beginning of your existence in the womb, and I'll be with you until the end of life on earth before you join me in heaven for eternity.

Sovereign Lord, how can You love a mess like me?

Ann, I do not create messes. However, I do create diamonds in the rough. In fact, I specialize in designing diamonds.

Then, Sovereign Lord, please teach this rough diamond how to cry. I could use a tear flood. And while you're at it, I need to learn how to laugh.

<u>S</u> Settling,
<u>E</u> even
<u>R</u> resting,
<u>E</u> every
<u>N</u> night to
<u>E</u> eventually learn that You never leave me.

THE TENSION

CHAPTER 4

As the Ceiling Fan Turns

How long, O Lord? Will you forget me forever?
How long will you hide Your face from me?
—Psalm 13:1 (ESV)

Most mornings, I dragged my weary body out of bed, clawing my way up to zero. Focusing on taking each breath that was weighing me down, my fatigue was getting the best of me. Feeling so exhausted all day made me yearn to go to bed long before dark, even if I couldn't go to sleep quickly.

I glanced at the clock often after supper. *Is it too early to stretch out?* This was my silent thought as I looked at my watch every thirty minutes, starting about six o'clock each evening. I realized that sleeping was an escape mechanism, but I didn't care. I just wanted to forget how difficult it was to live in my skin. Sleeping provided a brief respite from my debilitating existence of being desperate to breathe.

In addition, I was never a napper, which made the weekends difficult. At least I could get in bed, watch a 1940s movie, and attempt to forget my health struggles. I could get lost in another drama other than my own. However, that wasn't the worst part. I dreaded waking up every night around one o'clock and staying awake for several horrendously slow hours.

I would glance at the clock on my nightstand and want to cry (if only I could). If these walls could talk, oh, the pain they would tell.

"I need to cry but need to breathe even more," I grumbled.

What was God thinking? Not again. Not another night of misery. I screamed silently, so as not to awaken Al, who was a light sleeper. *Both of us don't need to be miserable.*

As the ceiling fan turned slowly, I lay on my back and had a variety of talks with God. My tone didn't surprise Him. After all, He had heard my distress many times. So once again, I started our conversation with more of the same:

What is the point of this, Lord? I know Your plan is to teach me, but what am I to learn? Can't I have one night of not waking up? You know full well that I have a speaking engagement tomorrow. I need to rest. It seems cruel to keep me awake for hours, but every night is a bit extreme. I feel despondent all day. Can I not have peace during the night?

As the fan turned, my thoughts went round and round. And when I dared to look at the clock, only fifteen minutes had passed. I snapped my head back in frustration with each quarter-hour increment. The fan was still twirling on the ceiling while I was still tossing in the bed.

Would someone pluck me off the ceiling? I'm holding onto one fan blade by the hair of my chinny chin chin. Wanting to catch my breath, I realized this was my issue: my breath was constantly shallow; this wouldn't give me a break, and it was no way to exist.

I would think of Bible verses like, "How long, O Lord, how long?" but my loose translation of the verse during this painful process became, "Seriously, Lord?" My prayers hit the ceiling as well as the fan. Or so it seemed.

Why can't I cry? If I were a crier, I surely would be crying. Instead, I stewed in my pity pot and stared once again at the fan blades. *When will this nightmare end?* Still watching it turn. Still watching it. Still watching. Still.

Why does the fan never stop? Or my frustration?

Finally, about five in the morning, I would drift off to sleep. Arguing with the Lord exhausted me, and I needed to save what little energy I had for breathing, shallow though it was.

Next thing I knew, I heard Al turning on the shower in the bathroom. The clock read 6:30 a.m. *Not again.* This not-going-away suffering felt overpowering.

I had to begin another day. In addition, that speaking engagement was this morning. The night of torment had already worn me out. Surely, one morning I'll wake up to find that this has all been a nightmare and that I'm normal Ann once more.

How long, O Lord? I resentfully mumbled part of Psalm 13 as I threw back the covers in disgust, crawling out of bed. I was ready to drop, and the day had just begun.

This wasn't for the faint of heart. My lack of breath was all-consuming. *I wish I could cry.*

God Chair Journal Entry

Sovereign Lord,
I don't have any energy left today. I'm certain You can tell.

Ann, just sit and rest with Me. Sometimes words aren't needed. Remember that when you are weak, I am strong. In fact, you are at your best when you are dependent on Me for everything, even your breath.

Thank you for being my Wonderful Counselor (and leading my path to godly, earthly counselors), my mighty God (yes, Jesus loves me; I am weak but You are strong), and Prince of Peace (You are my Peace Provider).

Thank you, Lord, for sitting here with me and just allowing your little girl to rest in You.

Ann,
I make you whole by filling the hole in your heart.

<u>W</u> When
<u>H</u> heaven
<u>O</u> opens my heart with a deep
<u>L</u> longing for
<u>E</u> eternity with God.

CHAPTER 5

Are You Hibernating, God?

Not on your life! Israel's [and Ann's] Guardian will never doze or sleep.
—Psalm 121:4 (MSG)

Of course I knew God doesn't hibernate. Everyone knows that—especially me, having grown up in the home of a pastor. But He made human beings survive by breathing, and I wasn't surviving well.

I couldn't breathe, and I needed help. "Energetic Ann" is now exhausted Ann. "Out in the front Ann" is now isolated Ann. Every morning, I awoke to the sound of my all-too-familiar shallow breathing (or was it my last gasp?).

Rough and tough resilience. That had always been me. But I was wearing down fast, like a grandfather clock that no one has wound up. Would the clock stop one day, and would I stop too? That was a wonder too hard to wonder, so I didn't.

Before I received an official diagnosis, I barely wrote anything. I knew, on an intellectual level, that it might help my emotions, but I had no energy to pick up a pen, much less write a single word. I didn't even know how to express my pain to myself, much less to God. Everything in my life had become confusing. Where would I even begin?

Somehow, once a month, I managed to jot a few tired thoughts in a journal. I usually wrote one or two sentences, which was all I could muster at the time. Here are a few of my entries:

February 2016
You know how weary I am …

March 2016
Why, oh Lord, is this breathing problem continuing?

May 2016
More than the healing, Lord, I want to know You on a deeper level.

June 2016
I am about to give up, Lord. *Help!*

July 2016
Every breath is such an effort. You know how I'm struggling.

August 2016
There seems to be no answer, and I am exhausted.

December 2016
This ship is about to sink with me in it.

January 2017
Tired of waking up tired!

June 2017
This was my last day at Choices, after twenty-five years, and I was too weak to enjoy the surprise lunch. Sad. I wish I could cry.

August 2017
Lord, You know what's wrong with me, so … *What is wrong with me?*

October 2017
Not sure how much longer I can do this!

November 2017

It's almost Thanksgiving, and right now I don't feel thankful.

Sometimes, I exhibited hope. Other times, I exhibited weariness. Mostly weariness. At times, I felt myself about to go off the rails. Then survival mode kicked in.

I was in hand-to-hand combat with someone or something every moment (sometimes it was with myself).

I was waiting, but when would my healing arrive? Or would it? There are no promises in life, after all. And that's another question. Why can't there be? I wrestled with Him.

Lord, I know You aren't asleep because You don't sleep. Still, I yearn to escape this dismay and disarray of emotions that I feel. I can't be brave much longer.

Or can I?

God Chair Journal Entry

Sovereign Lord,

There's a reflection of the candle wick that's on the coffee table. I see identical flickering flames bouncing on the deck. What are You wanting to teach me?

Ann, the two flames show that the closer you get to Me, the more you resemble My flame that lights up a hurting world to give people hope.

Sometimes you need to hurt first before you can give others My hope. Reflect on that.

You are slowly learning more about how to reflect Me, just by being with Me.

Lord, why don't invisible wounds heal as fast as visible ones?

Ann, I am using you, rest assured. Don't focus on your missteps. Focus on Me, always.

F̲ Forever
O̲ open to watch God
C̲ claim the
U̲ ultimate, eternal
S̲ success.

Lord, would You just give an uppercut to this breathing issue and send it on its way?

CHAPTER 6

Jesus with Skin On

I know the sorrow, and I know the hurt would
all go away if You'd just say the word.
—MercyMe (David Garcia, Ben Glover, Crystal
Lewis, Tim Timmons), "Even If"

God, send me someone who is going through a difficult health journey. I need to vent, share, and pray with someone who gets it.

This was a prayer of my heart. Although I never uttered it aloud, He heard the cry of my pain. And He plopped her into my lap in a drugstore, of all places.

Having known each other slightly at one time, we struck up a conversation that night. We each had heard that the other was embracing the pain of unresolved physical issues. We only talked briefly but heard each other's frustration loudly.

As I got into my car, I felt a God-nudge to text her and see if she had an interest in meeting for coffee.

Then I argued with God. *Lord, I can't do that. She is much younger than I am. Would she even want to hang out with a wrinkled woman?* I took the risk.

She responded, "YES!" to my text, and our confidential relationship began.

God revealed to each of our hearts that we could share confidences. He does that, you know. "It's in the vault, Ann," Becky, an old friend from my past, would tell me, when I shared something with her that was only for her ears—and God's.

The vault is always safe. One less thing to wonder about and be confused by. My new friend and I were going through a muddy time of turmoil, which sometimes felt like quicksand.

This caring millennial ordered two necklaces and gave one to me. My eyes teared up but wouldn't fall down. The words were simply stated, yet they meant volumes to both of us.

"And if not, He is still good" (Daniel 3:18).

We were praying for each other's healing on earth, yet if He chose not to meet our request, we were confident that He was still good. Few people believe that. God sent me one of them. I thanked Him for bringing her to me.

Sometimes, we simply meandered slowly through her neighborhood and said little. Just enjoying the sun and the Son. Other days, we were so weak physically, mentally, emotionally, and spiritually that we fast and furiously vented to each other. It was in the vault, and we felt safe.

Most of the time, we valiantly attempted to be superwomen for our families. But when it was just the two of us, there was no need to bolster our energy and plaster on a strong face.

Isn't it comforting to distribute some of the weight we carry in a crisis with people who become Jesus with skin on?

"What a blessing You have provided for me, Lord," I prayed often in gratitude. "You knew that I needed her." Staying in sound mind was a premium when living in a whirlwind of emotions. I knew that He was able.

I was confident that the journey, no matter how convoluted, would lead to the destination God had planned. He loves me that much.

I often wore my necklace, clutching it and reciting Daniel 3:18 whenever I was about to fall apart. On my worst days, I wondered if He was still good. She and I would sometimes default to the ploys of the deceiver.

Realizing we were human, she and I reluctantly accepted that we weren't superwomen, after all. Could peace and pain coexist? Absolutely.

During these three years, I witnessed some crazed moments. At times,

I was part of the insanity; other times, thankfully, I clutched lucidity, holding on for the long ride. God is in it all, I would recall often.

Remembering that small victories were huge successes, I hung onto the promise that He who was faithful would do it. Isn't that what 1 Thessalonians 5:24 taught me? I would cling to that knowledge engraved in my childhood.

She and I decided that superwomen we weren't, which was why we raised the white flag and conceded to leaning on our Super God.

Super God, take us away!

God Chair Journal Entry

Sovereign Lord,
I believe that You are at work even though I can't see the fruit of Your work right now.

Ann, you can trust Me.

- I am sovereign over your breathing issues.
- I am sovereign over your heart issues.
- I am sovereign over your bruised hurts.
- I am sovereign over your past regrets.

You name it, and I am sovereign over it.

I am sovereign over each member of your family, all of your friends, and the people I send to you as their burden bearer.

Remember something very important:
Do not be more than a friend.
I repeat. Do not-
I am their God.
Just remind them of that.

Yes, Sir. I will do so.

B Brutally
R ripped
O open for
K kingdom work and
E eternity with Him Who
N never ends.

CHAPTER 7

"Shhh ... Don't Wake the Children"

And he [and Ann] said, "I heard the sound of You in the garden
and I was afraid, because I was naked and I hid myself."
—Genesis 3:10 (ESC)

We all say, "Shhh ..." when our children are asleep. After all, naps for the little ones are, for the most part, so the big ones can take a break (or doze awhile too).

Our son and daughter were adults when my health volcano erupted, and we had two small grandchildren.

Lord, help me keep most of this away from them. I was serious, and God knew it. I didn't want to let them witness a pitiful Mama, Mother-in-Love, or G.G. (Grandmama Gainey).

Surely, I can pull these two items out of my bag of tricks for one more visit: the mask of smiles and a bundle of pretend energy. Or perhaps not. I wondered that and more as I made the almost-three-hour drive to visit our daughter and her family.

As I rounded the mountain curves, *The Little Engine That Could*, a children's book from years gone by, reminded me of my lofty goal: "I think I can. I think I can."

I yearned to sit on their sofa and do nothing. It was so soft, compared to the rock-hard seat in my car, where I wasn't only on the edge of my seat but seemed to be dangling off the edge of a cliff.

On their comfy back porch swing, I could escape into another world, a calmer space, a world of feeling better for a change (if only for a moment in time).

They chose a panoramic view for their new home. The landscape of the Tennessee mountains from that vantage point was to die for, and only God and I knew how close I felt to death.

Suddenly, I felt a jerk that dragged me back to reality. My car had gotten me to their home. I knew I had to pull into the driveway, whether I had the intestinal fortitude for it or not. Deep breath, Ann. But could I take a deep breath?

"Come on, G.G. Let's play Sharks and Minnows." The grandchildren saw a smile they thought was genuine. I was getting quite good at concealing my exhaustion. It was easier to fake it with little ones, who were so excited about life. If only I felt excited about living.

"G.G! It's your turn to be the shark."

Ann, you can be the shark one more time, I counseled myself, clenching my teeth. My TMJ jaw pain told me otherwise.

I think I can. I think I can. Or am I fooling myself?

I quickly became my own cheerleader; no one else had to know it wasn't real. With a master's degree in social work, Mary Katherine probably had a clue that I was suppressing a lot. She just didn't know how much, and she wouldn't, if I could help it. I could feel another, *I think I can. I think I can,* arise from the depth of my soul. *I wish I could cry.*

Perhaps I could win this game, without revealing my genuine state of despondency.

On the trip home from those majestic mountains, I would text Al about my estimated time of arrival. That gave him enough time to prepare himself for my grand entrance—or was it to be my finale?

Sometimes I didn't know whether I was coming or going. Living a topsy-turvy existence was no fun.

Where are tears when you need them? I mused. *How much longer can I keep this facade up?* My current life had become a pretense, a masquerade, an illusion. Could I keep the false Ann going? And if so, for how much longer?

I felt myself coming back to reality and my new normal of perpetual exhaustion. I despised the truth that I wasn't satisfied with what my life had become. Although I could hide it fairly well most of the time, I was incapable of changing it.

But the days had been fun for the grandchildren. That was all that mattered for the moment. *Mission accomplished,* I thought with a modicum of happiness.

I was making memories. I say that often to members of our family. It's like my signature, and hopefully they will say it when I'm gone. I'll be smiling from heaven. Perhaps sooner than I thought.

I was leaving Chattanooga. It was bittersweet, but I could now collapse inside myself. All pretenses could drop. I don't have to smile in the car, and no one is asking me to play. The walls of my car became my protection. Now, I could be the real Ann. No one can see your pain when you are alone in your car, except maybe yourself. And God.

God, can hiding away from others heal? Or is it just peaceful to hide when you aren't healing and don't know when you will get healing or if you will ever get healing on this side of heaven? And the beat goes on.

I chuckled to realize that I was old enough to recall Sonny and Cher singing that tune on television. She was tall and thin. He was short and had that unforgettable mustache.

"The beat goes on, the beat goes on.

Drums keep pounding a rhythm to the brain.

La de da de de, la de da de da."

When I got out of my car back home, totally spent, I threw my tired body onto the bed, with my clothes still on and my suitcase still unpacked. Al said nothing. Sadly, he knew that this was my normal now and lovingly gave me the space I needed. As I fluffed my pillow, sank into the mattress, and channel surfed for a 1940s movie, I wearily repeated the conclusion to *The Little Engine That Could.*

I had read it to our children so many years ago when I was young and had energy to play and could breathe without wearing a mask of merriment. *I knew I could. I knew I could.* Would I ever feel good again, like Ann once did?

Holidays and birthdays came and went. They are supposed to be fun and energizing. Why aren't they? My desire for healing took on the textbook effort of a firstborn.

I think I'm concealing the pain rather well, I proudly thought, to my demise. Was I fooling myself?

They say, "Mama is strong," "G.G. plays with us," and "Mother-in-Love encourages our family."

That is correct. It is what I do. And I would keep up the faulty front at all costs. I felt consumed with keeping my head and mental faculties above water, for myself and for each of them.

I think I can. I think I can.

I wouldn't allow my family to know the bitter truth about how fast and how deep I was sinking. The boat had a leak, and I was determined not to let them locate the place that was weak. *I can do it without crying.*

Perhaps I could replace the hole in the boat with the strong will that I had possessed since childhood. Hear me roar and make a joke at the same time.

That has been one of my roles in life. I make people smile. And that made me smile. Most of the time. But not now.

I have cried numerous times without shedding a tear. What I really wanted to do was cry. Only I couldn't. Or was it that I wouldn't? I wasn't certain of the correct answer, if there was one to be had, during this test of my will.

One answer was obvious. I was uncomfortably out of my comfort zone, yet making people smile was the pattern of my life.

Of course, I make people happy. No matter what.

Remember how stoic I can be?

I yearned to be rowdy and let out a no-holds-barred scream but remembered the mantra: "Shhh. Don't wake the children."

God Chair Journal Entry

Sovereign Lord,
What were You trying to teach me today?

- That you can trust Me.
- That you never have to fear sharing your feelings with Al or others.
- That I created you to be calm and rest in Me as your normal.
- That I can make you be bold and caring at the same time.
- That I created Ann to be real, not to wear a happy mask for stuffing pain.
- That I love you to heaven and back, just the way you are.

Consider it done, Lord. Things are shifting inside of me, and You are the reason. I do rejoice in that. Remind me that no one is invincible, but that I am strong in You.

CHAPTER 8

The Perilous Pontoon

Late that night, the disciples were in their boat in the
middle of the lake, and Jesus was alone on the land.
—Mark 6:47 (NLT)

On many occasions, I have been a little woman with a Titanic spirit. Some say that I lived close to the *Titanic* when it sank, although contrary to popular belief, I wasn't a passenger. I was, however, a passenger on the lake of lunacy.

Not breathing can make you feel a little crazy. So along with going to Tennessee and putting on a happy face, I could do the same locally as well with Elliott and his girlfriend.

Our son has a pontoon boat. Spending time on our local twenty-six-mile-long lake brings a smile to his face. An outdoorsman, he is. Jessica is too. They hike, bike, and enjoy two huge dogs. The dogs could overtake a room, and that was my plan.

I could hide my exhaustion when the dogs were around. They were so energetic and enormous that no one noticed me. With the dogs being the center of attention, I didn't have to make anyone happy. I could fade into the woodwork.

More relaxation. No stress. Less pressure. Ahh. Peace.

Elliott and Jessica took us out on the lake for a sunset ride. Then they took us to a restaurant on Lake Sidney Lanier.

We had fun on the tranquil ride. Elliott derives pleasure from driving his pontoon. I like watching him smile, so I wasn't concentrating on the lake.

The ride back from the restaurant was soothingly smooth. At first, that is.

In a matter-of-fact voice, Elliott broke into the silence. "See up there?" He pointed with the confidence of a ship's captain. "We are heading into rain." Due to his unruffled tone, I was naively convinced this would be fun.

I had never been in the rain, on a pontoon, going fast. It's true that ignorance is bliss. I saw the rain ahead of us and smiled at how enjoyable it would be to drive into and then out of the rain. After all, isn't liquid sunshine wonderful? It replenishes the earth, says God's Word. I enjoyed reading in our home by a window with a cup of tea in my hand, listening to the pitter-patter of gentle rain drops. That was a glimpse of how this ride home would turn out, I glibly thought.

But that daydream was not meant to be. This was a pontoon, after all. And the rain was a-comin'. Jessica implored us to move under the canopy, looking as if she had been to this rodeo before. Still oblivious to what was about to ensue, I remained relaxed, listening to and observing the rain. Elliott sped up, and I tensed up.

Jessica was calm as she motioned for Al and me to move beside her. I sported my favorite visor, and Al had on a Clemson University cap. We were unaware of what was about to transpire. The visor and the cap flew off in concert, taking a nosedive into the water.

What was happening? My breathing was getting worse with each passing moment.

Elliott was attempting to drive us quickly through the rainstorm. Obviously, I didn't know the meaning of "quickly." Al and I were handed a beach towel, though I wasn't sure why. We were under the canopy, after all, so what was the worst that could happen?

Well, it happened. The faster Elliott drove into the blinding rain, the more we felt blinded, literally. Now I understood the reason for the towel protocol. The rain was pouring into our faces like stinging swarms of bees not to be denied. I signed up for a relaxing pontoon ride; now I was in a war with rain bees. I felt ready to lose the battle, but hopefully not the war.

That's how I felt every day on this perilous path of battered breathing. I was ready to lose it any day, and the thought of drowning seemed a blessed relief. Then I wouldn't have to work so hard to breathe because the battle would be over. And I would be with God, the lover of my soul. I attempted to peek above the now-drenched towel.

How could Elliott see through the blinding rain? *He is an Eagle Scout,* I mused, trying to calm my nerves. *All is well.*

Each time I pulled the towel down an eye-width, I squinted to look at Elliott. His face was resolute. He didn't flinch. He got us to shore.

After we returned to the land, I asked how he drove with such ease.

Unflustered, he responded, "I've done it before." The lake didn't overtake him because he had experience. It served him well. And us too.

As Al drove us back home, I had much to think about. A variety of emotions swarmed like bees in my bonnet as I breathed shallowly.

Lord, I've never done this before, not breathing, I mean. I don't have experience on the lake of lunacy. Yet, You have placed me in it. You love me, I thought. *I'm confident of that, Sir. Yet I don't have a clue about what You are up to. I feel as if I'm treading water, and I could even be drowning. Have You noticed?*

Jesus, I know You are in the boat with me, but when will I be rescued from the swarming bees during this breathing storm? I'm waiting, but it's so hard. Are you watching?

Even if there is to be more blinding rain, help me remember that You have me in the hollow of Your hand in the security of Your ark of safety.

May I merely touch the hem of Your garment? You are my Rescuer from the torrential rain that incorrect breathing can cause.

This breathing boat appears to be going nowhere. If this is a cruise, drop me off at the next port.

Do you notice that I'm about to capsize? Where do I sign up for the balmy Bahamas?

After all, I just want to breathe.

Captain, will I weather this thunderstorm? Are you listening?

God Chair Journal Entry

Sovereign Lord,
You gave me a precious time over lunch with friends. We are each "going through something," as Karen Peck's song reminds me.

"Everybody's Going through Something"

> Everybody's goin' through something.
> Everybody faces a storm now and then.
> So if everybody's goin' through something,
> I'd rather go through something with Him.

> Storms come and waters rise
> and everybody cries.
> It's part of livin' while we're livin' down here.

Ann, I know when life storms are going to hit. You can weather each storm by holding on to Me. Peace in the storm is available to you as well. Reach out and receive My peace that the world can't give.

You are calming my storms and stilling the waves in my life.

In my God chair, I drop my anchor into the sea of serenity, anchored to Your stillness.

Ann, keep your focus on Me and not the waves.

CHAPTER 9

Trials, Temptations, and Tests

I have tested you [Ann], like silver in the furnace of affliction."
—Isaiah 48:10 (MSG)

[My dear Ann,] do not be surprised at the painful test you are
suffering, as though something unusual were happening to you.
—Peter 4:12 (GNT)

During the many months of health decline, I wondered, *Trial. Temptation.
Test. What do they each mean?* I decided to clarify those words.

Trials are times of anguish sent to grow us closer to God. This was a
rigorous time of anguish, to be sure. *Well, God, I never asked for this trial,
and I don't want it, so take it away, if you please.* It didn't please Him to do
so. It was a time of anguish.

Temptations come from our yucky flesh. *I'm tempted to give up, God.*
It was too difficult, and I wanted off this slow boat to China. He wouldn't
stop the boat for me to hop off. That seemed cruel, even though I knew
that He wasn't.

Tests are sent from God to see if we will obey Him. Exodus 17:7a
(NLT) reads, "Moses named the place Massah (which means 'test')." *I
know that You tested a myriad of people in the Bible, but why this particular
test for me? You could have chosen an easier row to hoe, Lord.* He knew I
wasn't a farmer. I crossed my arms, dug my shoes into the red Georgia clay,
stomped my feet, and complained like a three-year-old, "This test is not
fair." He just nodded, in His understanding sort of way.

I implored of Him, *Why me? I'm now retired after many years of ministry, Sir, and ready for my next assignment from the Master of my life. I have work to do for You. Why are You slowing me down?*

Giving me a God-wink, I clearly saw a smile of understanding from Him but felt confusion in my heart.

Then it hit me. I was in a terrible trial, a tempestuous temptation, and a testy test, all rolled into one.

Why would you gang up on me, Lord? I should have known that sulking didn't work with God, but it somehow felt called for. Although I knew better, I felt justified in pitching a fit. My situation was painfully prickly, and I was covered by masses of prickly pain brambles.

One day, while I was driving, I asked God why He wouldn't allow me the freedom to bypass this uncomfortable health journey and turn right into complete healing. It wouldn't have taken Him much time. He could snap His fingers and do that for the little girl He loved. So why wasn't He providing what I demanded? Baffled, that's how I felt.

I enjoy reruns of *The Andy Griffith Show.* Only the black-and-white episodes, of course. Everyone knew Opie's hair was red, so who needed proof?

One afternoon, while watching good ol' Andy (who I always thought looked like my handsome daddy), Barney Fife said, "We've got to nip it, nip it in the bud." He was quite adamant. You know Barney.

Well, I said to God, *You could nip this in the bud right now. So why won't You?*

I was now an actor in *The Andy Griffith Show,* minus the red hair. The director didn't have to tell me what to do. My arms defaulted to a stubborn crossing once more. I think He, not Andy or Barney, just smiled again.

The episode ended, and I turned off the television. Humming the well-known tune from the show, I wondered if I could move to Mayberry, where life was simple, and no one had breathing issues.

God Chair Journal Entry

Sovereign Lord,

I'm on the deck again. It's fun to have my God chair outside. What a difference a day makes. Yesterday was sunny, and today is overcast and breezy. I can tell that the rain that was predicted over the next few days is about to come dripping in.

Send the rain down as You reign over my life.
You send the rain to cleanse the pollen away.
Your reign over me cleanses my heart's impurities.

You test me through the droughts in my life and flood me with healing rain at other times. And You reign through it all. You know whether I need a test "to grow me" or a soothing rain "to drench me of pain" as a respite from it all. Either way, I'm beginning to trust You in a way I never have before.

Yes, Sir, I yearn for a rain jacket from Your throne to march through this health storm and a peace blanket to place over me for a safe covering until the breathing storm subsides.

Ann, in your chaos, I provide calm.

C Constant
H hurt and
A anger that
O only my
S Savior can heal.

C Coming in courage,
A always to the throne,
L lingering with my
M Master.

Lord, I choose calm.

THE TRIBULATION

CHAPTER 10

It'll Do You Good

It feels like an ocean of sorrow is under my skin.
Even the ocean eventually meets with the sand.
Sorrow on sorrow, I'm waiting.
Heavy, I'm anticipating.
Trusting the current will carry me.
—Leslie Jordan, David Leonard, Sandra
McCracken, "You Hold It All Together"

I despise waiting rooms, and I was in more of them than I could count during my breathing safari. They all looked the same: stark; cold; uncaring.

My appointment was at two, and by 2:30 there was no end in sight, just like this continuing health saga reveals no end in sight. Time drags on in waiting rooms.

Mama told us three children that it didn't take any intelligence to be on time. She was right. What is with you people, anyway? Don't you know we are sick? You are making us worse as we wait. Do I have to let out a wail in order to move to the front of the queue? If that will help, I can bellow with the best of them. Frankly, I'd rather eat a peanut butter and jelly sandwich at home than wait in line for a table at the finest restaurant in town.

Doctors' waiting rooms are the pits. And so was God's waiting room, I was to learn, once again. I had been in His waiting room many times before, but I'm older now, and this time, it may never end. Or so it seemed. *I cannot think of a worse place to die than in a waiting room*, I ruminated. Or was God just pulling comic relief on me. If so, it wasn't the least bit humorous.

Lord, I'm forever waiting for this appointment as well as for You to show up and heal me. Did you hear me? Are You listening to my supplicant cries? That is biblical, by the way. I remember that from the days of my youth.

Pastor Daddy would be proud.

I had to force myself, through clenched teeth, not to organize a mutiny on the Bounty with the others in the waiting room. There were more than enough of us to gang up on them. Feistiness was rearing its ugly head, and I had my sword in tow.

With a devious gleam in my eye, I thought, *I'm a leader and know how to put a plan together. Someone needs to promote change in this waiting room. Give me a microphone, and watch me whip this ship into shape. All for one, and one for all.*

The following week, passing the time as I waited in yet another doctor's waiting room, I grumbled and had a pity party. That was easy to coordinate these days: A pit pity party. Say that three times fast. I was tired of being in the pit of despair.

Was I bummed? No. I was angry. *What makes me think this doctor is going to give me a diagnosis? No one has yet. And the chairs aren't comfy, and I don't like what's on the television. The HGTV Channel again. Is this a conspiracy? Or am I just that frustrated?*

Thinking of Mama again, I recalled things from my childhood to pass the time. I was back in my teen years, hearing her voice: "Ann, go mow the grass and get a tan at the same time. It'll do you good." That was back when a tan wasn't a skin cancer concern.

Well, if Mama was in this waiting room, I'm convinced she wouldn't say, "Enjoy the wait for a diagnosis, Ann. It'll do you good." She would come up with a plan, fast.

Where was Mama when I needed her? My brother, sister, and I knew that when Mama put one hand on her hip, we were in trouble. But when she placed both hands on those hips, we had better beware, for a sermon was a-comin'. She was a take-charge woman. I got that quality from her.

"Mama," I said in desperation as I glanced upward to heaven, "I wish you were here with your hands on your hips, straightening these people out. You know how tired your little girl is."

Why did God take you so soon? I need you, Mama.

"Ann Gainey," the nurse called, "this way."

God Chair Journal Entry

Sovereign Lord,
Why must I continue waiting?

Ann, waiting is just Me activating good things in you internally.

<u>W</u> Willing for God to
<u>A</u> activate a perfect
<u>I</u> internal
<u>T</u> time frame for my life.

Ann, waiting is a wonderful wilderness.

What is wonderful about waiting, Lord?

Ann, in the wonderful wilderness,

- **you learn to rest,**
- **you grow as never before,**
- **you stop striving and start relying, and
  you learn of Me in a way that is fresh.**

And in the wonderful wilderness, you appreciate the value of small things that are oh, so huge to your heart.

Lord, thank You for this wonderful wilderness, ordained just for me. And I will wait on Your perfect providence.

CHAPTER 11

Don't Tell Me I Look Great

And I could tell it was going to be a terrible,
horrible, no good, very bad day.
—Judith Viorst, *Alexander and the Terrible,*
Horrible, No Good, Very Bad Day

"**D**on't tell me I look great." That's what I wanted to scream at them. They were such kind people, trying to encourage me, and I knew their heart was to help. So I stifled the scream that I wanted to blare out in a not-so-sweet tone and splashed on a grin instead. "You are so kind," I said aloud. We do that in the South, no matter what. May I add that we are quite convincing. It's called practice.

"I'm dying on the inside," is what I wanted to retort. But I worked up a quick smile and, with an extra tablespoon of Southern kindness, calmly replied, "Thank you for caring."

Women say that so well. I was a Southern lady, after all. We know how to smile and stuff at the same time. *Why don't I look as bad on the outside as I feel on the inside, Lord? Then they would be quiet.*

Feeling quite fragile emotionally, I felt anger toward the people who walked by me each day. At work. In the grocery store. Even the post office. They look well. I feel sick. They appear not to have a care in the world. I want to vomit my pain on all of them. That doesn't sound kind or Southern, I thought, so I squelched that yearning, pushing it deep down, yet again.

They all seemed so peppy. I, on the other hand, was pathetically pouty (on the inside, that is; I wouldn't let the world see my heart's pain).

Would I heal on earth, or did I have to wait until heaven? *If it is to be heaven, Lord, I want to go there sooner than later.*

Mama would love to see me. I haven't touched her since 2008. I watched as she took that last breath before leaving our family. Thank you for that gift, Lord. I asked You to let me be there at the moment when she left us and relocated to her real home. You graciously provided. I did cry then, the entire last six days of her life on earth.

"I miss you, Mama. And I need you to hold me like you did when I was a first grader at recess and tried to jump off the side of the school porch over a mud puddle but didn't make it. Or as a married lady after major surgery. You stayed two weeks as I mended, taking care of our son and daughter while I was in bed, healing. Why can't you be here now when I need you even more?" Quite often, adulting is not pleasant at all.

I didn't want to go to church or social events because of the one question I would always hear and dread: "Are you feeling better, Ann?" I got tired of playing make-believe. For as long as I could recall, I was the one who would light up a room with joy. Now I ran from people because I didn't want to answer that dreaded question.

Keep breathing and smiling, Ann. That had become my daily, personal slogan. Sometimes the façade worked. It was like playing dress-up as a little girl. But those happy, youthful memories were long in my past. Pretending was a farce that I wasn't certain I could continue ad infinitum.

Remember that stiff upper lip.

So when asked if I felt better, I sang the same old song in the same old tune: "No, I'm not any better." I had to squelch the urge not to include, in a not-so-happy tone, "Stop asking me that."

Ernest Hemingway hit the nail on the head when he said, "You are so brave and quiet; I forget that you are suffering."

God, You are taking too long. And I've waited soooo long. Why is this happening?

I was going into a shell and becoming a recluse. That wasn't Ann. Ask anybody. Survival became my middle name. My heart was leaning toward hardness, while my face exuded happiness. Could I keep this charade up forever? Probably not.

Why didn't someone, anyone, say, "Ann, you look awful." That would have blessed my heart. But the fact was that I didn't look awful. All the pain I experienced was internal, not external. And even if I had looked bad on the outside, people who care about you yearn to be an encourager. I've said the same thing to others. Maybe one day, I'll be brave enough to say to a friend, "You look awful. Do you want to share your pain with me?"

People usually leaned on me during their tough times. Now Ann was becoming harder to find. *Where have I gone?* I reflected silently. No one answered. I wasn't surprised.

Lord, I just want to stay in bed and watch black-and-white movies from the 1940s. Life was simpler then, like a walk in the park.

If only these gentle people knew how sick I felt. They heroically tried, to no avail. Al couldn't comprehend it fully, and he was with me every day. Begrudgingly, I understood. All of a sudden, a line from a song from the 1960s, sung by the Essex, came to mind: "Easier said than done." I chuckled as I sighed.

There is a presentation today, Lord. I have to breathe. I need to smile. This is important. I can't afford for anyone to see my pain. I feel lost in the shuffle of what my life has become.

And the feeling is ugly.

I don't look so good.

God Chair Journal Entry

Sovereign Lord,
I'm hearing a bird tweet, "per-ty, per-ty, pert-ty."

Ann, I am reminding you that you are beautiful to me just as you are. You are "pretty, pretty, pretty," so you don't need to compare yourself to anyone.

That's a freeing reminder, Lord.
You promise to love me just as I am, yet you love me too much to leave me where I am.

"It's Beginning to Look a Lot Like Christmas" (my version)
It's beginning to look a lot like freedom
everywhere I go.
Take a look at the grass and sky,
watching me say, "Oh my,"
and looking at creation differently.

It's beginning to look a lot like freedom,
calmly enjoying life.
And the thing that will make it ring
are the birds that daily sing
right within my heart.

CHAPTER 12

I Can't Sing

It's easy to sing when there's nothing to bring me down.
But what will I say when I'm held to the flame, like I am now?
—Mercy Me (David Garcia, Ben Glover, Crystal
Lewis, Tim Timmons), "Even If"

Mama sang to us three as we were growing up, yet I became the one with the musical gift from God. Early on, I played the violin, the harp, and the piano. Yes, the concert harp that my daddy and another man carried the two city blocks to our church in downtown Columbia, South Carolina, so I could play for the Christmas service. They caused quite a stir walking across four lanes of traffic. I didn't understand the significance of that harp performance at the time, since I was only eleven.

I took piano lessons for twelve years. In high school, I played important roles in several Rogers and Hammerstein musicals. In the ninth grade, I was in the Gilbert and Sullivan operetta, *HMS Pinafore*. These lines are indelibly marked in my memory: "All that glitters is not gold. Black sheep dwell in every fold. Things are seldom what they seem. Skim milk masquerades as cream." How was I to know those words would make sense years later?

These words from high school resonated in my heart during this health issue. Shallow breathing wasn't gold, nor was it skim milk masquerading as cream. Ugh. Life is tough, but God is tougher. I had learned that now, oh so many years later.

Awarded a voice scholarship at Erskine College, I sang in the elite chorus known as the Choraleers and in the musical *Flower Drum Song.* Suffice it to say, music and drama made me smile.

"Hear ye! Hear ye! Let it be known to all who read this that it's impossible to sing if you can't breathe."

During my thousand-day journey, I mouthed the words to the songs at church each week, not wanting people to know I wasn't singing. Perhaps it was a fake-it-till-you-make-it mentality. Was I wrong to do that?

Perhaps it was a way not to allow people into my pain. That got old fast, which was one of the many reasons I dreaded Sunday and church and people in general. You don't miss your arm until it's in a cast. You take your leg for granted before it breaks. I thought my breath would always be there, until it wasn't.

And when I turned on a Christian radio station in my car, I was silent. What a deluge of disappointments. When my body was weak, my emotional health shield became weak, so I folded into myself for protection. Unbeknownst to me, my shoulders slumped a little more each day. Eventually, I was staring at the ground instead of looking toward the sky, at God, my Help and my Redeemer.

God, why have You allowed this voice that You placed in me, meant to praise You, to vanish? He was silent. I knew that the God Who loved me so deeply would do nothing that was cruel. He didn't hate me. The Bible told me so. I learned that from my childhood.

Then, why, Lord, would You, during this long breathing issue, remove something that was so vital to my happiness? My voice and my love of singing.

Silence again. Surely, there was a reason.

My mind was mangled and mushy. I knew Psalm 150:6a (NIV): "Let everyone [including Ann] that has breath, praise the Lord." Why could I not rejoice?

I knew that the joy of the Lord was my strength, but I had little air left in my lungs to thank Him for the depressing drama He was playing out in my life.

I can't find my voice, God. It is long gone. Why? I trust there is purpose. I know that You make no mistakes, but please give my singing to You back. You are able. I implore You to work ... now.

My breathing prospects seemed bleak at best, unconquerable at worst.

What would happen next in my life movie? This certainly is not a merry musical with energetic choreography.

I wanted to run away. I couldn't escape my breath or God's breath because then I would soon run out of breath entirely. And that was me right now.

Oswald Chambers said, "If the devil can hinder us from taking the supreme climb and getting rid of our wrong traditional beliefs about God, he will do so. But if we stay true to God, God will take us through an ordeal that will serve to bring us out into a better knowledge of Himself."

All I wanted to do was sing to Him. Doesn't the Bible talk about praising Him with psalms, hymns, and spiritual songs? Was that too much to ask? I decided to make a valiant attempt one more time.

I cleared my throat.

I opened my mouth.

I was ready.

Nothing came out.

God Chair Journal Entry

Sovereign Lord,
I sing these words to You.

To the tune "Great Is Thy Faithfulness" (my version)
You are my Rescuer,
Oh, God my Father.
There is no shadow or turning with Thee.
Thou changest not, Thy compassions, they fail not.
As Thou hast been, Thou forever wilt be.

Lord, not only did you rescue Al when his vintage 1968 Cutlass flipped over and Elliott in his devastating truck accident, but You rescue me from myself daily. You have rescued me even when I didn't know that I even needed a Rescuer.

You have been my Provider even when I didn't know what my need was or that I even had a need of provision.

Ann, that is the truth. My truth.

I can "live in Your light" so I don't have to "be in the dark." You never turn Your face from me. Thank You for being constant and never changing. You are so compassionate.

Ann, your breath has never been your own.
It is My breath in you.
Now, breathe Me in.

CHAPTER 13

TMJ Too?

> How long, O Lord, will you look on and do nothing? Rescue
> me from their fierce attacks. Protect my life from these lions.
> —Psalm 35:17 (NLT)

My TMJ challenges began thirty years ago, before I knew what those letters meant. I didn't know it was a fierce attack from a predator called the deceiver of my soul. For a week, I noticed that my jaws felt tight. *This is strange*, I thought. Then I woke up one morning and felt the crowning blow: I couldn't open my mouth more than a smidge. What's going on?

My jaws had locked, and I felt scared. Out of control. *What do I do? Not a comforting feeling.* I learned a lot. Fast. Faster than I would have liked.

Temporomandibular joint (TMJ) dysfunction is the lengthier name. What it means is great pain. That lingers forever. Or so it seems. Flare-ups came unannounced, like a lion suddenly released from his cage, prepared to pounce.

I didn't know what was coming down the track back then. The day I woke up with a closed mouth, that is. I wasn't sure where to turn. In later years, I was aware when the lion was about to unleash a fierce attack. When I was about to have a TMJ event, it would be obvious. Like a red flag, those tight jaws warned me. It was as if a vise was closing down. A relentless lion vise that wouldn't let go. I didn't understand God's plan for me then.

For years, I had been wearing a mouth guard at night. It was uncomfortable, but I had learned the hard way that many good things in the long run are painful for the moment. They can keep us from having to endure other issues. I rested in that knowledge as I faithfully placed the accommodating guard in my mouth each night, and rolled my eyes as Al joked about the high cost.

Off and on, during the many years of TMJ hurdles, I had episodes that would last a few months. I had learned the "vise prelude," what I had to watch for, and started babying my jaw during the day as well: soft food and jaw wiggling exercises. I knew the medical sequence all too well.

I recently asked my dentist why the episodes were closer together than before. He said, "Well, now you have arthritis in those joints too." Great: the aging process.

Dr. Phillips warned me, "When you wear the mouth guard, it allows one muscle to work so that the other muscles can relax." Guess I needed to be an obedient student, I surmised, reluctantly.

So it made perfect sense that I would continue to have episodes during my breathing health journey. After all, TMJ issues are so much about tension. I was indeed tense, all the time, except when I was asleep, which didn't happen often.

During this health debacle, my body became extra tense, and I couldn't get the jungle beast to settle down.

I was glad to keep that expensive mouthguard securely in place. It was eight hundred dollars' worth of serious security that forced my jaws to relax. I needed that at night. But during the day, my mind was in a vicious cycle of deciding which specialist was next, finding directions, fighting traffic to get there on time, and of course, spending time in the waiting room. It was a medical jungle every day. And the jungle was filled with tall weeds. And lions.

Of course, attempting to keep the happy mask on at work was becoming more of an effort. But Ann was trying. She always does. I saw more tension on the horizon. *Can I do it? I think I can. I think I can. Keep going, Ann. You are the survivor, remember? Buck up.*

My entire body stayed tense 24/7, just as my breathing remained shallow 24/7. Anxiety galore. A ferocious animal on every side. Now I was adding to my tension my usually acute (now chronic) TMJ. I was confused, to say the least, and disturbed. As well as perturbed. Which led to God-vents that sounded many times like this:

What are You thinking, Lord?

Is this a joke? This would be funny, except it's not.

Is the breathing problem not enough?

Why are you adding insult to injury?

I feel as if a hungry lion is pouncing on me.

Or perhaps, I'm imprisoned in a spinning hamster wheel from which I can't free myself.

Are shallow breathing and TMJ to be my new normal?

No more ferocious lions, hamster wheels, or metal vises.

I can't keep this facade going, no matter how hard I try.

I have had enough of it, already. If this is to be my lot in life, I am ready to go to heaven. I don't have to roll the dice for an answer. Yes, I choose heaven instead. On with it, Lord.

But He didn't give me that option. He just kept saying that four-letter word I had come to detest: "Wait."

I said, *Take this lion away. Put him back in the cage.* Only He didn't acquiesce, and the vise clamped down tighter.

Come to my relief, Lord. You see that I'm tense. And where did I put that eight hundred dollar mouth guard, anyway? The TMJ lion won't win today. Or will he?

I'm climbing a grueling mountain, Lord, with the mouth guard in place and ready for duty.

Are you not watching my plummeting plight?

The lion is fast approaching.

Come to my rescue.

God Chair Journal Entry

Sovereign Lord,
Thank You for providing medicine for my TMJ.

_T_ Turning
_M_ my tension over to
_J_ Jesus.

And then

_T_ Turning
_M_ my attention over to
_J_ Jesus.

Thank You for making me aware of the tension I carry in my body and for using my God chair as a reminder to be more attentive to You.

You are my Relaxant.

No prescription required.

You restore me.

Everything else is sinking sand.

CHAPTER 14

Frozen in Time

I have been in labor and hardship, through many sleepless nights,
in hunger and thirst, often without food, in cold and exposure.
—2 Corinthians 11:27 (NASB)

"God, quit pausing me on Your heavenly remote control," I said in a not-so-kind voice.

I felt frozen; our television does the same thing sometimes. It irritates me to a small degree but drives my Type A husband a little nuts when ours freezes for fifteen seconds. *Seriously, Al, fifteen seconds?*

"How would you feel if your life was frozen in time for over two years?" I yearned to say those words to my most-of-the-time sweet hubby … in a not-so-kind voice. But I stopped myself, midstream. Counting to 10 had helped. I sighed, glad that I had chosen well.

Patience, Ann. I'm tired of the *wait* word and now the *patience* word. Knowing the wisdom of picking our battles in marriage, I wisely defaulted to repeat several times silently, *Deep breath, Ann, deep breath.*

Then I realized that this was the problem. I had no deep breath with which to calm myself. I somehow managed to count to 10 slowly. That didn't work in the calmness department, either, but it would have to suffice for now. I had no other recourse. Will this whirlwind ever stop whirling?

One day, I'll be able to breathe again, I told myself confidently, with a tenuous smile. *Or will I? Am I fooling myself? Or is this another denial?*

Lord, I know that I heard You correctly about Your next assignment for me being a burden bearer for other people. So why have You allowed me to carry my own burden of illness for so long? You can see that I feel frozen in many ways. Thaw me now. I know You are able.

But I wasn't noticing any drips to indicate that the thawing process had begun. Still frozen in time. And no thawing in sight.

It's easy to do the wrong thing, say the wrong thing, feel the wrong thing. Life can feel so lifeless at times.

I indignantly muttered, "Well, I will just freeze my emotions so they can't hurt me." Knowing that wasn't logical or in my best interest, I did it anyway. My shoulders straightened appropriately, and I tensed intentionally.

After all, that was one thing I could control: hiding behind the ice of pain. I was so busy that I had forgotten how to twiddle my thumbs. How can I relax?

I knew, from difficult situations in the past, that there is no greater gift than pain, for it always sends me to the Pain Reliever: God. I also knew that the flip side of pain is opportunity, if I chose wisely.

Were all of these events providentially planned by the One Who loved me the most? We humans have difficulty processing what we don't understand. All I knew was that I felt as limp and lifeless as a Raggedy Ann doll.

I couldn't seem to see past all the pain. Would it end? The onslaught of doctor appointments and the mass of medical tests were about to do me in. I tried to strike a peaceful posture, but I would often ruminate on the reality that I might never get well. That thought was a bitter pill to swallow.

What was that music in my ear? I recalled and hummed the song that Annie sang from the musical of the same name: "You're Never Fully Dressed without a Smile."

With courage like Annie, perhaps I could continue to face each day, fully dressed with a smile.

Frozen. Smiling. Happy.

Or was I?

God Chair Journal Entry

Sovereign Lord,
Thank You for the snow that's still on the deck.

Ann, just as every snowflake is unique, so is every person. There will never be another Sydney Ann Beckham Gainey. I am creative that way. I am forever molding you into My image, and this breathing issue is one of the tools I am using to accomplish My plan for your life. Work with Me by "not working" so diligently. Relax. And watch Me work. I'll make it happen.

Lord, this song is in my ear: "Jesus, I am resting, resting in the joy of who Thou art. I am finding out the greatness of Thy loving heart."1

Lord, I feel like Raggedy Ann. The doll always had a smile. I wonder how she felt, deep inside. Hmmm.

You and Raggedy Ann can genuinely smile (inside and outside), knowing I am always beside you and inside you and all around you. You are safe.

I love You, Lord.

Love you more, Ann.
(We both smiled.)

CHAPTER 15

Not Knowing

If no one knows what will happen, who can
tell him when it will happen?
—Ecclesiastes 8:7 (NASB)

I despise not knowing. You too? It is tension producing. And I was, indeed, tense. Do you remember my TMJ issue from a few chapters back? I rest my case. My body, constantly tied in knots of not knowing, was weary.

I am standing before Your throne, Lord. That was my cry of frustration one day. I wanted to know what was wrong with my body. Adversity can be a blessing or a curse. Right now, it seemed more like a curse. Again, I spoke out my restlessness to Him.

In case You haven't noticed lately, it's an effort to breathe. My energy is below empty, and this constant fatigue is exhausting.

By the way, Lord, everything I do in life right now is debilitating. Check it out, kind Sir. Worn down to nothing, that's what I am. Nada. I'm tired of being tired. I'm weary of being weary. I'm sick of being sick. I'm not happy about not knowing. Have I made my point, Lord? I really hope You are listening and on the brink of giving me answers. I have waited for over two years. Isn't that long enough?

I was screaming, but no one seemed to be listening. I knew that God had to be listening, yet I saw no help in sight. And I was looking everywhere for some sort of solace. Why wasn't He giving me the gift of a diagnosis?

Have You even noticed that I can hardly take a breath, Lord? Seriously, not a productive breath. On my own. You know all things. You know what is wrong with me.

Yep. Not knowing is awful. My mind was reeling, and my judgment was failing. I was well aware that God created our minds to know Him fully, as we are fully known by Him.

The head knowledge, I had. After all, I was a preacher's kid. What I needed was for all that knowledge to travel to my heart. And fast. A change of perspective was necessary, and I was out of pep talks to myself.

I had gone through other tough times during my life, but I always knew what I was fighting. Clinging to God for help in time of need was my go-to, but this time, I didn't know what was wrong. Not knowing is *knot* knowing. My entire being was tied in knots and poised to quit.

To say that I was on my last leg with not having a diagnosis was an understatement. Perhaps I was bumping into the reality that I would never know. And if I never knew, I would never be healed on this earth. That was a sobering thought on which I chose not to dwell.

Could I wade through another not-knowing day, keeping my chin up and plastering another "Ann smile" on my not-so-content face? I wasn't certain that I was up to the fight. I was punching an elusive shadow. I want to know what's wrong and give it a name.

Lord, I'm in an awful abyss, I said one day. Wondering exactly what an abyss was, I did some investigating by way of the dictionary:

- a seemingly bottomless chasm (check)
- an immeasurable space (check)
- a deep void (check)
- emptiness (check)
- nothingness (check)
- a frightening situation (check)

Well, God, that just about says it all, except may I add that this is awful. I'm lying here, half-dead in bed, channel surfing for a 1940s movie. And I'm giving up.

God Chair Journal Entry

Oh Sovereign Lord,
Thank you for being sovereign over everything so I don't have to stress over anything. Lord, the color blue is especially soothing, and You've given me a blue sky with no clouds today. You are my Sovereign Soother, the Sovereign Soother of my soul.

The soft blue calms my mind, assists my concentration, and is mentally comforting. I'm in a serene state with my Sovereign Soul-Soother.

Ann, there is safety and security in being still. When you are still, it is easier for you to sense safety and security in Me.

Be still and know that I am God (Psalm 46:10a ESV).
Be still and know that I am.
Be still and know.
Be still.
Be … Be with Me, Ann.

Mama and Daddy would tell me to be still in church. And You are telling me the same about not knowing what's wrong with me.
I will be still and just be with You.

CHAPTER 16

Eeny, Meeny, Miny, Moe

Jehoshaphat was alarmed by this news and sought the Lord for guidance.
—2 Chronicles 20:3a (NLT)

The neuromuscular specialist didn't miss a beat when she said, "Your next step is Mayo Clinic." I was sad and glad, all at the same time. Sad that I had no diagnosis locally. Glad to hear that I should go to Mayo Clinic. Pronto.

I had to focus. Many people believe that Mayo is the greatest medical center in the world. People come from everywhere for a diagnosis and treatment in their facilities. Right?

My jaw was set (TMJ and all). The next assignment was clear. So *Eeny, meeny, miny, moe. To which of the three Mayos do I go?* Yet another decision. And I was weary of making decisions. But this was my next step, so I did some research. There were Mayo Clinics in several locations: Florida, Arizona, and Minnesota.

I decided to approach the closest one first. Florida would suit me the best, because we could drive there and be warm. I'm a cold-natured woman, after all. Reared in the South, remember?

Sadly, they didn't accept my case due to the long wait for an appointment and didn't keep a cancellation list. They knew I needed an appointment sooner. No argument from me on that.

We would have to fly to Arizona, but the weather wouldn't be too cold, perhaps. *I do live in Georgia,* I thought. *Weather is a consideration.* God created me, and I was raised in the buckle of the Bible Belt. It's not my fault. Blame it on the parents. Doesn't everyone?

The Arizona Mayo Clinic turned me down with the same logic. They knew finding a diagnosis was of high priority. I agreed. There was only one Mayo Clinic left to contact: Rochester, Minnesota.

By this time, I wasn't thinking about the weather conditions in the frigid winter of Minnesota. I wanted to get well and would swim the wide sea to achieve that lofty goal.

God, what if they won't take my case? It's the only Mayo Clinic left. I talked myself down off the cliff. *Calm down, Ann. Don't borrow trouble. God is in control.*

I answered when my cell phone rang in mid-November 2017. "Mrs. Gainey, we have received a fax from Atlanta indicating that they are referring you to the main Mayo Clinic here in Rochester, Minnesota."

My heart was pounding out of my breathless chest. At least they called me. *That means there is a chance.* I listened intently while I scrambled for paper and pen.

She indicated I would receive a form via email in the next ten minutes. Once they received the form back from me, I would get a phone call in two days. *Why the two-day delay for an answer? Ann, quit overthinking.*

The diagnostic team would determine if they would accept my case. She kept talking, and I kept scribbling her words, frantic not to forget anything. My heart was racing as I sat at my computer and waited. It was there. In ten minutes. Just like she had told me. As quick as a jackrabbit, I filled out each question and just as quickly emailed the form back.

It didn't take two days. In two hours, I received the phone call that she had promised. I was amazed.

"Mrs. Gainey, our diagnostic team has accepted your case." Were my ears hearing right? *This must be a dream.*

What? God had parted the Red Sea for His little girl. He loves me and ordains my steps.

Then I focused on her next important words.

"Now Mrs. Gainey, let's see when it would work for you to come to Rochester to be seen."

I was expecting the appointment to be in several months. I would have been pleased. I wasn't going to be disappointed in the wait.

Mayo is going to see me! Thank You, God.

"I'm retired now, so my calendar is quite flexible," I managed to say professionally, without squealing for joy like a little child.

"Well, how about December 6?"

December 6? Next month? I was in awe of God. *He allowed me to cross that ol' Red Sea onto dry land.* And December 6. It was mid-November now. *We could make this happen. Thank you, Lord!* I continued to write everything she said. This was an amazing feat from my amazing God.

"You will be at Mayo Clinic five to seven business days. Bring all of your medical records with you. Don't mail them ahead of time. We don't want reports of your MRIs or X-rays. We want the actual CDs."

Okay, I thought. *I'll do whatever this sweet Midwestern woman asks of me. I love cold Minnesota already. Focus, Ann. Focus.* She kept talking. I kept writing. I was still floating on an ecstatic cloud when we ended our lengthy conversation. This was surreal. Almost uncanny. Except I knew that God, my Provider, had provided. He loved me and was in this healing process. I had no doubt.

Al was the first person I called. He was at his office and elated to hear the almost unbelievable news. Then, I paused to thank God once more. I was doing my Jesus dance in our living room when there was a whisper, a still small voice. I wondered why God stopped my dance before Him?

"Ann, you thought that the main Mayo Clinic was your last choice, but it was My first choice for you."

I wasn't sure what God meant. *Was He speaking to His daughter, Ann? Or was I imagining?* I pushed the thought aside because my Jesus dance wasn't finished yet.

A few days later, the whisper that I had not understood before made perfect sense. Someone in the know mentioned to me that the Minnesota Mayo Clinic is the one you go to when you have no diagnosis. *Really? Was that person correct?*

If so, I hadn't known that. Nevertheless, God had, and He knew that was what I needed. A diagnosis.

God already knew what was wrong, and He knew where to send me. The doctor God had given the knowledge about my issue was there, waiting on me to arrive. In the frigid weather of Rochester, Minnesota. I laughed at God's humor but trusted His perfect ways.

December 6, 2017, was my first arctic appointment. My problem began August 6, 2015. *Hmmm* … Any connection?

He had created a cold-natured, Southern belle and was placing her in frigid Minnesota.

What was He thinking? Little did I know that the joke was to be on me. God had a sense of humor, and I was soon to find how much of a funny bone He had.

God Chair Journal Entry

Sovereign Lord,
Thank You for being You for me.
Now I need Your peace, Lord.

"Peace I leave with you[, Ann].
My peace I give unto you.
Not as the world giveth,
Give I unto you" (John 14:27a KJV).

P Pleading
E every day to God
A and
C calmly
E emerging a different person.

Lord, You give Your peace in my pain. What a relief and joy.

THE TRIP

CHAPTER 17

A Minnesota Mission Trip

So is My Word that goes out from My mouth: it will
not return unto Me empty, but will accomplish what I
desire and achieve the purpose for which I sent it.
—Isaiah 55:11 (NIV)

I retired six months before I went to Mayo. "Refired" is what I call it. Not because I was fired twice, though. Several friends thought it sounded that way.

My thought: If I'm not doing Kingdom work, God might as well take me to heaven now. That is why I preferred the term *refire*. Refired for whatever God's next assignment was for me. Except this breathing issue had derailed my perfect plan.

Time had marched on for well over two years, with no diagnosis in sight. Maybe I was going to Minnesota on a fool's errand. Just another disappointing dead end?

August 6, 2015, had been a day of disaster, as far as I was concerned. Could any good come of that day? Would I ever consider it a day of delight?

But God had parted the Red Sea, providing me a December 6 appointment. All was well with the world. Full court press was in order. Off to the races to gather what the staff at Mayo needed me to bring.

I rushed from specialist to specialist in Hall County and Atlanta, getting CDs of test results and copies of medical notes from each doctor. Years' worth of doctors' notations with test results in thick files. It took time and gas, but I didn't care. Mayo had accepted my case. I floated on a cloud for a week, praising my Boundless Lord Who had been sovereign over arranging this schedule at the most renowned medical facility that I knew about.

Just for me.

A nobody to the world.

A somebody to my Lord.

When, before my very eyes,

KAPOW!

BLAM!

ZAP!

Words from the *Batman* television show, with Adam West as Batman, rang through my ears as God gingerly plucked me off the cloud and placed me on my feet. I wasn't dancing on top of the clouds anymore. Why? Because the God of the universe wanted to tell me an important message from the depth of His heart. I stopped. My listening ears were on.

"Ann, I am sending you to Mayo Clinic in Rochester, Minnesota, for two reasons.

"One reason is eternally more important than the other. Listen carefully."

Believe me, I was all ears.

"You will receive a medical diagnosis at Mayo because I have gone before you and have given My expertise to the doctors. But greater than this is …"

I was waiting for a heavenly drum roll.

"I am sending you to Rochester, Minnesota, on a mission trip."

Then He paused, waiting for it to sink into my mind. What? Did I hear Him right? Perhaps I'm delirious with the excitement of getting an appointment. That's probably it, I surmised. But I was still listening quietly. Perhaps He would reveal more.

"Ann, you heard Me correctly. I do not speak in words you cannot discern. You know Me. So you heard Me."

What a different perspective; I got excited again, this time for another reason. Breathlessly, I managed to ask the question to be sure I had heard correctly:

Lord, You are sending me on a mission trip to Minnesota?

"Ann, I do not need to tell you twice."

I heard Mama's voice once more: "Ann, I told you once to clean your room. I don't need to tell you twice." I could see her hands on her hips. Were God's hands on His hips? If so, a sermon was a-comin'. And He had lots of practice preaching.

I was sure that God's sermons would trump Mama's sermons at home and Daddy's sermons from the pulpit, any day. After all, He is God.

What a massively different perspective I now had about my upcoming appointment on December 6. I did a Jesus dance again. This is exciting. No, exhilarating. "Exhilarating" trumps "exciting" any day. I focused on His plan, taking as deep a breath as possible.

This trip wasn't so much about my diagnosis now. Ann is not the one. God is the One. All for His glory. And I'll get to watch it unfold. In extremely cold Minnesota, with my coat and gloves securely on my cold body.

Lord, You have orchestrated every step of this health trail. I thought it was all about my illness. Turns out it's really Your plan to reach a hurting world. Starting in Rochester, Minnesota. Very shortly. You are sovereign over me and over every step that I take on this jumbled journey. I am honored that You chose me for this heavenly assignment. Humbly honored, indeed, Sir.

Lord, give me boldness. Keep my eyes open. I don't want to miss any opportunities. This will be a blast. A God-blast. Sitting back and watching You do Your job. Now my trip is less about Ann. I get it.

"He must become more important while I become less important" (John 3:30 GNT).

That verse came to mind in a way as never before.

Father in heaven, I am Your servant. This mission trip is all about You. I am on pins and needles, anxious with anticipation, Lord, to sit back and watch You work Your perfect will. I know that You don't need me, but I am blessed that You are choosing to use me and to grow me closer to You in the process.

This will be a fun extravaganza. I was wondering how He would work His plan yet had no doubt that He would.

A Minnesota mission trip. Who knew?

Oh, that's right, Lord.

You knew.

God Chair Journal Entry

Sovereign Lord,
I am looking at all the evergreen trees off our deck. It reminds me of a sermon title Daddy preached in my youth called "The Evergreen Christian." What does it mean to be evergreen?

Ann, it means being

- *ever ready (not to miss any opportunities),*
- *ever supplied (in Me you have everything you need),*
- *ever focused (on Me and not on the world),*
- *ever growing (in your walk with Me), and*
- *ever content (in the center of My will).*

Well, Lord, consider me Your "Eveready Ann," supplied by Your heavenly batteries, that never wear out, to keep me going.
An Eveready Ann … I like that name. It has a godly ring to it.

B Being
R ready
A and
V vibrant for
E every opportunity to brag on God.

CHAPTER 18

Up, Up, and Away

And now, compelled by the Spirit, I am going to Jerusalem
[Minnesota], not knowing what will happen to me there.
—Acts 20:22 (NIV)

Remember, my focus had changed, and God had changed it. I repeated
His assignment numerous times before the journey to Minnesota began.

"Ann, your diagnosis is second. My glory is first. Remembering that
will serve you well."

*Aye, aye, Captain of my soul. I don't want to miss any opportunities that
You place at my feet on this Mayo journey. The path of Your possibilities is
limitless.*

Little did I realize that the first opportunity would be placed before
my very eyes as soon as Al and I arrived at the airport in Atlanta. The first
person God put in our pathway was the baggage handler.

Glancing at our tickets, he asked with interest, "Why would you be
flying to Rochester, Minnesota? And in December?" Obviously, he had
grown up in the South too; we both knew the Southern drill. I didn't miss
a heavenly beat.

Smiling to my new friend, I replied with gusto, "I'm heading to Mayo
Clinic for a breathing issue that hasn't been diagnosed. And I'm willing to
be cold because God opened the door for me to get there."

Looking deep into his eyes to see if he would join in my praise, I
immediately noticed that his demeanor had changed. His face was intent,

and his words decreed the same. He lowered his voice and said with reverence, "He is a good God."

To which I replied, "I believe that life is too short not to brag on Him. And the older I get, the more boldly I acknowledge Him to others."

Now he was really into our conversation, not merely handling suitcases and getting a paycheck. "Preach on, little woman. The blood covers it all."

We exchanged some more God-talk, and he gave us a blessing as we left his church (I mean his baggage pulpit). How invigorating. God is going before us. All I have to do is open the conversation. He will do the rest. It's always His modus operandi.

"Remember that, Ann."

Yes, Sir. I rest, and You do the rest. What a deal You have for me. I just get the privilege and gift of watching You at work.

I was floating on a cloud as we got onto the airplane.

God, I plead for this to be a gentle, smooth flight. You know that turbulence is not my happy place. In fact, it's terribly terrifying for me. You have known that since the foundation of the world and don't need reminders. Your memory is awesome. Except when You choose not to remember, like my sins.

You are so good about that. Have I said thank you for that lately, Sir? He smiled.

The pilot came on the intercom to inform those of us who cared—that would be me—that there would be turbulence closer to Rochester.

Why? The pilot said that there were 35 mph wind gusts already in that area, waiting on a Southern belle named Ann to arrive.

I glanced out the window and asked God the proverbial question concerning the turbulence for almost three years of no diagnosis:

Why? And *Why me? Did You not hear my plea?*

He lovingly responded to my anxious heart, "Ann, any type of turbulence in your life gives you training to rest in Me."

Why are you always right? I wondered, yet I didn't think that was a question to ask.

I knew the answer. *He is God, and I am not.* What a relief and comfort to my somber soul. I tried to breathe as calmly as I could.

Off we flew into the wild, blue yonder. During the flight, I remained quiet, because there was much to ponder. Mostly the unknown. *Maybe*

Mayo can't diagnose me. What then? Ann, don't go down that rabbit trail. I talked myself off the plane's wing.

Al was reading. I joined him. Anything to pass the time until the turbulence arrived. A flight attendant walked by and said, "That must be a good book."

I was exhausted from walking through the huge airport and, as usual, not breathing well, so I said nothing but did manage to hold up the book jacket. The title was *Trusting God*.

She replied with a genuine smile, "Ah. It *is* a good book." I managed a weary smile back.

"You have a friend, Ann. Act on it."

I won't miss an opportunity, Lord. You and I are a team.

"Remember that. It will serve you well."

Later, she saw me looking out the window as a tear trickled down my cheek. She didn't know that this was sobbing for me, and I chose not to educate her on my tear history.

Yet, God propelled her over to me. She leaned over the seat and hugged me; she looked into my eyes and said in a gentle and sincere voice, "It's going to be all right."

God had sent her to me as Jesus with skin on.

Thank you, Lord. You always meet me at the point of my need. I clutched my Daniel 3:18 necklace and prayed for my friend back home who gave it to me.

As the plane landed, the pilot informed us that the temperature in Rochester represented a chill factor of minus 1. And it was midday. I cringed. But no turbulence. I smiled about that. God just wanted to develop my faith and trust muscles. That's my take on it, anyway. You would have to ask Him yourself to be certain.

As we exited the airplane, I told the flight attendant—now my new friend—that God had used her to minister to me.

I looked into her eyes and added, "God has great plans for your life."

As she returned my smile, I reminded her that God had given her smile as a great gift to her. "He is planning to use your smile to help many more people than just little ol' me."

"You're about to make me cry now. See?" She wiped her own tear away. I wondered if that was sobbing for her too.

I mistakenly assumed that my God-time with her was over, but as we hopped onto the hotel shuttle, looking for a place to sit on the quite full vehicle, I saw her sitting in the back. As God would have it, the only two seats left on the van were right beside her. God was just waiting on us to sit down.

As we walked toward her, I put my hands on my hips in the aisle, like Mama, and said aloud, for all in earshot to hear, "Seriously? Only God does this," as I looked into her eyes and smiled. I sensed she understood, too, that God was at work. The shuttle moved while she and I chatted. I asked about her family. They lived near Atlanta, and she had a husband and young children.

Sharing with me a tough decision she had to make soon concerning her employment, God opened another door. I walked through it as she was emptying her heart. God put the next words into my mouth that I knew were ordained just for her ears. I opened my mouth and His words to her flew out.

"I read a devotional twenty years ago that I have never forgotten. It has ministered to me over many situations," I said. "The devotional read, 'We often ask God for direction, which He will provide.'"

She seemed on the edge of the bouncing seat, focused and eager to hear the rest of my story.

"But He really wants us to ask for His wisdom, because then we get not only direction, guidance, and clarification, but all of what God has to offer, which is all of Him as well as all of His wisdom. Ask for His wisdom in this decision, and He will give it to you."

I stopped talking. God was finished using me for the moment. She thanked me.

I may never see her again on earth. My guess is that our mansions in heaven just might be side by side. What a nice thought. He does cool things like that.

When we got to our hotel room (which was to be our home away from home for the next ten days), I anointed everything with oil that a friend had given me.

An anointed room. An anointed Ann. The room, as well as Ann and Al, were ready for the next part of this journey.

Standing in the hotel room, I felt so many emotions: anxiously nervous, anticipating with excitement the unknown, timidly timorous about the outcome. But with Al holding my hand and God holding each of our hands, I was certain that whatever happened would be okay. Even if we went back home with no diagnosis.

I clutched the necklace and repeated those words, "And if not, He is still good."

Thy will be done, Lord. Thy will. Thy strength. Thy guidance. Thy wisdom. I choose not to wonder what tomorrow might bring or speculate as to whether a diagnosis is in my future or not. I rest assured in Your power and am confident that You are holding my future in Your mighty hands.

With the reminder that we had all of His wisdom, Al and I prayed together and slept in peace.

Wonderfully exhausted.

God Chair Journal Entry

Sovereign Lord,
I yearn to hear from You today. To be Your willing warrior is my heart's desire.

<u>W</u> Wanting to

<u>I</u> initiate

<u>L</u> loving the

<u>L</u> lost

<u>I</u> in

<u>N</u> never-ending Kingdom work with

<u>G</u> God at the helm of my ship.

Ann, are you ready?
Do you have your seat belt on?

Yes, Lord. It is on, and I am your ready servant.

Then Ann, let's join hands and start this exciting journey.

CHAPTER 19

Anxious First Day

> This is the day the Lord has made. We [Al and
> Ann] will rejoice and be glad in it.
> —Psalm 118:24 (NLT)

I say that verse before I get out of bed at home; I almost forgot that I wasn't in Gainesville, Georgia. I said Psalm 118:24 that first morning in the hotel room and for all ten mornings while there. It was automatic. That's what I do.

During my lengthy breathing issue, I even added my own verse to the ritual: "This is the day the Lord has made. I [Ann] won't dread anything in it." That was a reminder to myself for over two years that for one more day,

- I would not dread another specialist,
- I would not dread another day of straining to breathe,
- I would not dread being the tired cheerleader at Choices Pregnancy Care Center,
- I would not dread my situation, wishing I were at home with the covers over my head,
- I would not dread wearing the mask of happiness, and
- I would not dread adapting to my physical weakness.

It didn't always work. But it helped. I was desperate. Desperate for God to show up and show off. And I was grasping to hold on to any words that would keep me treading water, so that I wouldn't drown. I didn't have time to drown. There were too many things to accomplish.

Ann, remember:

Not dreading.

Keep treading.

Not dreading.

Keep treading.

That was my morning mantra at home. I could transfer that to Mayo Clinic. No. Mayo was going to diagnose me. God had given me a peace about that. In addition, I was on a mission trip. *Remember that, Ann.*

So why was I so anxious the first morning of my Mayo appointments? It was December 6, the day long-awaited. I wasn't expecting this reaction. Ann is in control. Ann is excited about being at Mayo. Until this morning. I was having this conversation with myself while Al was in the fitness room. It was good to be by myself, alone with my thoughts and holding onto my God before the first day of appointments began.

I softly sang aloud some of the lyrics I recalled from "There's Something about His Name," an old tune by Bill and Gloria Gaither. When my breath would allow it no more, I sang silently. I wasn't certain of the reasons why that song came to my mind but knew that God had orchestrated it. I also was convinced that recalling the words to that song was His wonderful attempt to calm me down. After all, there would be back-to-back appointments today. I would be strong and steady. I had to be. Could I locate some steel nerves in the hotel room for added security? I had practiced being strong for sixty-seven years. I could do it in Minnesota too. My branch was bending, but my trunk was strong.

But what if no one can diagnose me here? Then what? "Stop, Ann." Mama would say that to me. I needed her here and Daddy too. I had my husband. I wanted my parents along as well. You're never too old not to want your parents by your side, especially during difficult times.

Daddy, in his nineties, had organized tons of people to pray for me. It was difficult for him, watching his eldest child sick. He was healthy and prayed the same for me.

I'm certain he was wishing he could switch places. That is what daddies do. And husbands. But neither of them could. Some crosses are meant to be borne alone. I knew that, and they did too. So they prayed. Intercession is a blessing.

In fact, Martha told me that one day, while praying for me in her living room, she felt God lead her to stretch out on the rug, prostrate before Him, crying out for my healing.

I would have thrown the burden to anyone for a while if I could have. Many would have shouldered my burden. After I finished singing the song, I anointed my forehead with the oil that a sweet friend had given me for the trip and read Psalm 91 aloud. Then I skimmed through the commentary on the chapter.

The introduction in my New Living Translation Study Bible included a theme and a preface:

"Theme: God's protection in the midst of danger."

"Preface: God doesn't promise a world free from danger, but He does promise His help whenever we face danger."

The author was anonymous.

The author could be me, I surmised, as I contemplated the theme of potential danger. The danger of never healing until heaven. That sounded like danger to me. I thought that but hesitated saying it aloud.

Well, I'm in danger, or could be, if Mayo can't figure this out, were some of my thoughts. I returned to my reading: "Those who live in the shelter of the Most High will find rest in the shadow of the Almighty" (Psalm 91:1 NLT).

Hmmm. If I live in His shelter, I'll find rest in His shadow. I meditated on that as I talked to my Lord. Then I continued reading all sixteen verses. He gives me peaceful promises in His peaceful presence. I kept reminding myself of His peace as I got dressed. I needed that reinforcement from His Word.

Biblically energized, I thought I was ready to go, until I realized that it was 16 degrees outside, with a chill factor of zero. Quickly I added my long johns to the attire for the day. I attempted to sing loudly, hoping that would provide more steadfastness of heart. The song of a few years ago, sung by Meredith Andrews, came to mind: "Spirit of the Living God." It was difficult to sing, because of my shallow breathing. My favorite line, for such a time as this, was, "Come now and breathe upon our hearts."

Now I'm ready, I told Al, who had showered and dressed as I had read and sang. My godly armor was in place. And I was prepared for any danger, foreseen or unforeseen. Precarious balance: That was me. I felt like a horse at the starting gate, raring to go.

We had breakfast, and then I put on my earthly armor. Boots, two pairs of gloves (yes, two), two scarves (yes, two), super warm coat. I already had the long johns on, as you recall.

The hotel shuttle took us the short drive to downtown Rochester. I saw the Mayo Clinic sign and thought, once again, how blessed I was to be here. To even walk through the doors. Mayo was world-renowned, I had read. *Thank you, Lord.*

Quaking in my thick, heavy boots, we walked into Mayo Clinic. God had opened the door, and now I was literally walking through it. They don't accept all cases, I reminded myself. God parted the Red Sea. They chose Ann. No. God really chose me. Be glad. Not anxious. But the building was huge, with seventeen floors. Subways take you from building to building, I had heard, and it was true.

We had no idea where we were that first morning. Eventually finding my first appointment, on the seventeenth floor no less, I checked in at the front desk and sat down, eager to catch my breath.

Sadly, I was used to that.

I was too nervous to organize a mutiny. Much too tired for that. Jet lag, I supposed. My toes were tapping with uncertainty. I quietly waited, holding my four-inch binder of two and a half years of files, tests, reports, doctor's notations, and CDs of MRIs and X-rays. I kept the notebook securely on my lap. It was my refuge, as was God.

I couldn't lose it, this notebook. The files were my proof, part of my awful life for way too long. But I was told to bring this entire notebook, and I was ready. Prepared. Armed and dangerous. An organized firstborn. Ready to fight the good fight.

I wanted Al with me at each appointment. I needed him to take notes as I answered questions of each doctor. This was our plan. Divide and conquer. We were of one mind. Having flown this far, we couldn't miss a word.

"Ann Gainey?" We got up quickly, following obediently and compliantly. The entry was a typical medical hallway, as was the exam room. A kind woman took my vitals. She left, and we waited once more, with silence between us. "God, calm my racing heart."

A knock on the door broke the silence. Although I wondered who was behind the heavy door, her smile and caring countenance quickly put me at ease. And it helped that Al was sitting beside me, poised and prepared to take notes. I was appreciative of that vital role he was playing. One less thing about which to think. Breathe, Ann (or try to breathe).

Since I had no diagnosis, Mayo had placed me with a general internist first. That made sense. I took a breath (or tried to).

She asked why I had made the long flight to Rochester. Holding my huge notebook in my lap like a security bear, I told her my medical saga while she listened intently, without interjecting a word, her eyes intense. When I got to the end of the story, she took a breath of her own and began asking a myriad of questions.

"What was your job before you retired?"

I explained the position I had held for twenty-five years. She then asked the sibling position in my family.

"I am a firstborn."

"Tell me about your parents and siblings."

I rattled on, answering each question as best as I knew how. Why was she so interested in my family background?

She then asked Al to step out of the room while she gave me a brief physical exam, asking me more questions. Where was my note-taker? In the waiting room. I needed him by my side. Jesus with skin on. Come back, Al.

My note-taking husband returned shortly. The doctor looked at us and smiled. "I have been practicing medicine for twenty-seven years in four different countries. I know exactly what is wrong with you."

The doctor's words were concise and confident. How could she know? And this quick? Certainly not. I had only been in the exam room for forty-five minutes, and she gave me a diagnosis? I was happily skeptical.

It helped that I had every test for every disease, that had to do with breathing, already performed in Georgia. She knew what I didn't have after I explained my medical menagerie.

Of course, the diagnostic team had to concur, so we had six and a half days of appointments left.

We tried not to get excited and wouldn't tell our family yet. After all, she could be wrong.

On the other hand, had we stepped into a miracle at Mayo?

Time would tell.

God Chair Journal Entry

Sovereign Lord,

You are my
Protector, Provider,
Rock, Fortress,
Deliverer, Rescuer,
Good Shepherd, Healer (body, mind, soul),
Shield, Helper,
Redeemer, Lifter of my head,
Sustenance (who keeps me alive),
Breath,
Alpha, Omega (beside me at the beginning and until the end),
Light (in my dark times), Salvation,
Forgiver, Sustainer (when floods overwhelm me),
Comforter, Soul Keeper,
Perfecter of Ann, Risk-Taker,
Strength, Interpreter of Truth,
Joy, Peace,
Rest, Restorer,
Master, Victor (in my battles),
Lion and Lamb,
Friend till the end,
Boss of me.
You are enough because You are my everything.

Ann, you bless Me and make Me smile.

CHAPTER 20

Mayo Put Me First

Pleasant words are like a honeycomb, sweetness
to the soul and health to the bones.
—Proverbs 16:24 (NKJV)

I was treated like royalty at Mayo Clinic; I felt like Queen Ann. There is a story behind my being Queen Ann when Al was the Hall County Commission Chair. But I digress.

"May I help you?" I turned around. To whom was she speaking? I hadn't asked for help, but I'm certain I looked frazzled. She wanted to be of assistance, so she put me first. But they put all of us first. Everyone was special at Mayo.

It started in the late 1800s. Mayo Clinic, I mean. Their first clinic. Right where we were standing. The two Mayo brothers were doctors. Settling their families down in the tiny town of Rochester, Minnesota, one of their first priorities was forming a value for their small clinic.

"The needs of the patient come first." That strong value continues to resonate even today. God made it clear to me that at Mayo I would bless others, and others would bless me. I was happy for both to happen but often felt as if all the blessings were showered just on me. If this was all a dream, being at Mayo, I didn't want God to wake me up.

There was a serene feel, and nothing smelled sterile or medical. In fact, I rarely saw personnel wearing medical garb, and I mentioned that to Al. My theory was that their goal was to keep the patients and their families calm and mentally intact. We needed that.

Al and I felt stressed. That's why we had made the trip to Mayo, so serenity was at a premium. The staff innately sensed that tension and accommodated us at every turn. In fact, they oozed kindness. Did they know how they soothed my anxious soul? When we looked in a tizzy for the next place to be, *what floor? which doctor?*, they reached out to support us. The staff always watched for confused faces, so they talked with us frequently.

Hustling and bustling from appointment to appointment wasn't a simple endeavor, yet they made it seem so. Even when we weren't asking for guidance, they noticed our distraught faces and stopped us to help. "You look as if I might be able to assist you with something." We smiled a sigh of relief, graciously accepting their information, jotting notes so as not to get lost again. Mayo's value spoke loudly everywhere we roamed. We, indeed, felt like deer and antelope, as the tune suggests, but we weren't playing. We were down to business.

A different retiree volunteered to play the baby grand piano in the atrium each day. Properly positioned to resonate throughout the mammoth seventeen-story building, the piano tones soothed the hearts and calmed the nerves of all of us. The needs of the patient came first, yet again.

At the end of an especially difficult and lengthy day, a woman in pink sat down on the bench at the baby grand. I couldn't take my eyes off her delicate and nimble fingers as they lovingly played "Jesus Loves Me," "Faith of Our Fathers," "Away in a Manger" (it was December, after all), "Swing Low, Sweet Chariot," "To God Be the Glory," "Amazing Grace," and many other songs of comfort. *They think of everything that our hurting hearts need.*

I teared up. What a blessing to listen and feel comforted while waiting for our hotel shuttle. I prayed for all who worked at Mayo and for the life of the Mayo brothers, long gone, but forever remembered. They had thought of everything that our hearts and minds needed.

Then came twenty more minutes of music to soothe our weary souls. I secretly hoped that our van would be delayed. *Were Al and I in heaven instead of Mayo?* Another gift from God. I sang aloud softly for as long as my breath would allow me the pleasure. Then I sang silently. God heard both forms of praise and smiled. I guessed that He was joining us in song and maybe His angels as well.

Because I was triple-layered dressed, the cold air could only nip at my cheeks as we made a fast walk to the hotel shuttle when it pulled up in front of the clinic. The needs of the patient come first. The needs of Ann came first too. I meditated on that sentence during the short drive to our hotel. Everyone at Mayo truly lived those words out.

I felt so humbly grateful that my eyes started to glaze over. Was a tear about to pool out? That would be another miracle.

In fact, I couldn't put Mayo Clinic into words. God is awesome. A number of years ago, a friend had told me to use the word "awesome" only in reference to God. It's truth, and I've passed that wisdom on to others along the way of life.

Food is good, but not awesome. That word is reserved for God only.

Mayo Clinic? Fabulous.

God? Awesome.

He is the mysteriously Mighty One.

And believably awesome.

God Chair Journal Entry

Sovereign Lord,
What do You desire for me?

Ann, I yearn to give you these things:
Calmness
Comfort
Relaxed muscles
Less tension
More contentment
Happy laughter
Freedom to breathe
All of Me (less of thee)

You have to reach out and accept those gifts.

"I will sing of the mercies of the Lord forever.
And with my mouth will I make known Thy faithfulness,"

What marvelous "mercies of the Lord" you have bestowed to our family.
Mayo. Wow. Who would have guessed I would be here?

So with my mouth I will make known Thy faithfulness.
No more missed opportunities.
Especially at Mayo.

CHAPTER 21

It Has a Name

When a train goes through a tunnel and it gets dark, you don't throw
away your ticket and get off. You sit still and trust the engineer.
—Corrie ten Boom

It was functional breathing disorder, or so I thought.

That is what the general internist had said.

Triggered by the trauma of that minor medical procedure several years
ago. It seemed like forever, I mused silently. *There has been nothing simple
about this health journey.* Before my diagnosis, often my lips would utter
I cannot fight what I don't know I'm fighting. It would usually be delivered
with vigor, a tad of anger, and TMJ tension through a clenched jaw.

Now I knew, and it had a name. The procedure happened August
6, 2015. On December 6, 2017, at my first Mayo appointment, I could
verbalize it aloud. No more flight. It was time to fight.

But wait. Was the general internist correct in her diagnosis? This
wasn't an engraved-in-stone confirmation, and my time at Mayo was just
beginning. Many other doctors would confirm or reject her diagnosis.
Don't get overly excited yet, I reminded my racing heart.

A chest X-ray was next. Followed by the pulmonary function test
(PFT). Another test? I've been up to my neck in tests for way too long.

*I have had about five PFTs. So what's one more? I'm confident that I'll
pass with flying colors. In fact, I could give the test to myself with one hand
tied behind my back. But I'll choose not to argue. This is Mayo, after all. They
are my boss right now.*

There is nothing wrong with my lungs. We know that. I never thought there was. Why? I had never had a breathing challenge in my sixty-four years of life. The shallow breathing began right after that medical procedure, so it was a no-brainer. No lung problem. Even non-medical Ann could surmise that. Case solved. Let's move on. My firstborn leadership ability was about to kick in, but I wisely squelched the inclination.

During a pulmonary function test, there is a nine-minute break between the individual tests. The techs had left the room for a breather themselves, so I was using the time to pray, making spiritual use of another wait. Hands open. Palms up.

When the techs returned to the testing room, one of them saw my prayer stance, looked at me, and said, "Meditation is good."

I answered, "Well, I was praying. I believe that nothing comes to me until it is first sifted through the fingers of God before it reaches me." No missed opportunities.

The older and wiser tech quickly replied with a knowing smile, "And I agree."

The other tech remained quiet yet seemed interested in our conversation. A seed was being planted. The Lord was using me and would send others to water the seed. The test continued, and I was following all their instructions, as an obedient firstborn pleaser would.

"God's got this," I said over my shoulder, smiling as I hustled to my next appointment.

Glancing at the crumpled schedule in my now-nervous hand, I looked at Al. What floor is next? What building is it in? Will we be late?

With no time to spare, we located the next appointment on the correct floor, and I breathlessly took my seat as the instructor began to talk. "Let me show you how to work the overnight test; it will identify breathing irregularities."

A woman was explaining the directions to an encircled group of us, handing each person a small apparatus. This would be my overnight friend. Another test. I was taking notes once again, wondering where Al was when I needed him. I gathered the instructions and all the parts that went with the small machine. I met up with Al in the waiting area, and we made our way to more appointments and then back to the hotel.

Whew. Having shallow breathing made everything harder to accomplish. But I made it through the day.

Fasting began at 7 p.m. for the next morning's blood draw. We weren't adjusting well to the time change from Eastern Standard to Central and so went to bed early. Worn out.

Meticulously, I positioned everything for the sleep study, hopped under the covers, slipped the finger clip on as the instruction sheet noted, and willingly closed my eyes. No one had to rock us to sleep.

Before I heard Al breathing hard, I managed to give him a quick "Good night. Sleep tight. Don't let the bed bugs bite" before I heard him breathing deeply. *It must be nice to go to sleep that quickly,* I thought, as I tried to drift off. Although exhausted, I managed a prayer first. God had followed us through all the day's appointments. I was lulled to sleep each night, reviewing the day.

Thank you, Lord, for walking alongside us today. Help me sleep with this apparatus on my finger.

Al was breathing even deeper.

How nice it would be to breathe like that, I contemplated. Hopefully, one day, I can breathe well too.

Is it selfish and ungodly to be jealous? I didn't answer my question before I saw the sheep jumping over the fence.

Actually, the Mayo doctors were the sheep, jumping as I counted. I asked God to bless each one and then rested in the Lord's capable arms for the night.

Zzzzzz.

God Chair Journal Entry

Sovereign Lord,
I'm watching the sunlight shining through some of the magnolia leaves but not all of them. Why is that?

Ann, My will is that My light shines through every person to show Me to a hurting world, but not everyone has yielded enough to be okay with that. They either don't know Me well enough to share Me or they are fearful to share Me. Both reasons sadden Me.

Lord, may I never hold back from letting Your light shine through me and then out to others.

May they see You ... not me.

I recall Will Rogers saying. "Go out on a limb. That's where the fruit is." I concur, Lord; no missed opportunities for me.

Lord, may I always go out on a limb to share Your love to those in need of You.

CHAPTER 22

The Cross before Me

The world behind me. No turning back. No turning back.
—Simon Marak, "I Have Decided to Follow Jesus"

That's the way I went to sleep one night and how I woke up, to that old but familiar and comforting song. I felt unrestrained and happy when I sang, if my breath cooperated.

We had to get up extra early for the 6:30 a.m. blood draw. Because of the dark, I saw it. Clearly. At five o'clock, in the murky twilight of the almost daylight. I opened the hotel room curtains and to my surprise witnessed another of God's gifts to my heart. This gift was luxuriantly luminous, melting my tired body with renewed joy.

It was a large cross high over a church in the distance. Out of our window. God even designed the cross in my favorite color: turquoise. He is so in the details of loving me. It was illuminated. In the dark. His light to wake up my overtired soul.

I strained my eyes to look above the cross into the still dark of early morning and whispered, "Thank You," to the One who sent it. "You love Ann," my shallow breath uttered. God was winking at me through the stars around the cross.

Smiling more confidently than when I first woke, I focused on Psalm 91 again, reading slowly to absorb His words into my spirit. Then I recalled from my childhood the verse about God's Word being a lamp to my feet and a light on my path. Today, His lamp would light my path to Mayo Clinic. Another "Thank You" was in order.

After Al had breakfast (I was fasting), we headed to Mayo via the hotel shuttle, as usual. I adorned my chilly body with heavy clothing and boots, once more, as a proper Southern belle in the frozen Arctic would do. Is blood even flowing this early? Surely, I'll be at the head of the line.

The vast majority of the people at our hotel were Mayo patients. All was very quiet on the dark ride that morning, making me realize that I wasn't the only one who had lots of agitated thoughts. I looked into the faces of each person, wondering about their journey here.

For some, cancer.

For others, heart issues.

For me, functional breathing disorder. If that was, indeed, the correct diagnosis. *Do not overthink, Ann. Just keep putting one foot in front of the other. Trust that God is at work, even when you can't see the fruit.*

We entered the clinic front door; a helpful staff person directed us to the blood draw floor. Surely I'll be the first person in the queue, since it's so very early, were my hopeful thoughts. Rounding the corner, I didn't expect the view, and my blood froze.

There were tons of people waiting for a needle zap, all sitting in rows of a hundred or more chairs. How early did you people get here, anyway? I wondered if they had seen a turquoise, lighted cross first, or if that was just for me?

I wonder how much blood Mayo draws in a day. Even though it was early, I needed some comic relief.

However, as usual for everything at the clinic, the line moved rapidly. After all, remember their motto: The needs of the patient come first.

The phlebotomist was out for blood: mine. It didn't take long. As I left, I gave her a December message of "Have a blessed day and a Merry Christmas." I didn't get a response back, although there was a smile; another seed planted.

Next on today's schedule was a breathing class. Not needing any directions, I chuckled to myself as I made my way to the correct floor. Needing some more levity, I mumbled thoughtfully.

People, have y'all ever heard of a non-breathing class? Do you even understand the "y'all" colloquialism? I need the class for non-breathers. Sign me up for that one, if you please.

Good thing that I chose not to verbalize all my thoughts. I'm guessing the instructors might not appreciate my attempt at a joke. Glancing at my trusty watch, I realized that it was still early, and perhaps the ever-so-nice staff had not downed their stiff cup of caffeine yet. As for me, I drink decaf because of my bones. Osteopenia.

I'm glad God gave me a sense of humor and a glass-half-full attitude toward most issues. It has served me well throughout my life, especially the exceedingly rough spots. Like now.

A kind woman (everyone is kind at Mayo) worked me in for my next appointment. Hooray for her and for God. I told her that God had used her as an answer to my prayer. True to form, I bragged on God all through that two-hour appointment. *Woo hoo. We are on a roll, God. No missed opportunities for me.*

I was about to meet my soon-to-be-favorite medical person at Mayo. Little did I know the depth of that blessing at the time. Although I was oblivious in the waiting room, God was about to give me another surprise gift.

When I would go to any new appointment at Mayo, I would say to the staff person, "I am a Christ-follower and believe that nothing comes to me that is not first sifted through the fingers of God before it gets to me. So I know God is using this medical issue for my good because He is always for my good." I got a variety of responses, which didn't bother me. I was being faithful.

To my surprise, this counselor's eyes got large. Leaning over her desk, she responded with glee, "I'm so glad you said that." My heavenly Guide through Mayo, as well as through life, opened the discussion door so that the rest of our lengthy visit was God-focused. And most delightful and insightful. Just like Him. It was fabulous to be in the middle of watching Him do His job, yet again.

At the end of the short (it seemed to me) two hours, Deb said with a strong yet gentle voice, "There's a book in you." We were on a first-name basis now.

I was shocked by her words. She gazed intently into my eyes and paused, in order for me to contemplate her words and let them soak into my soul. On autopilot, I glanced at Al, confident that I would see his grin. He had encouraged me for years to write a book or at least some devotionals. Yep. Grinning he was.

I actually started a devotional, to please him mostly. I wrote twenty-five devotions. They are still in a notebook upstairs at our house. Buried in a box somewhere, I would guess.

Deb pulled out her business card. "I'm writing my cell number on the card. Stay in touch with me as you progress down your healing road." I guessed that she didn't give out her personal number very often.

As the appointment ended, I asked her if I could pray. As the words to God began to exit my mouth, I felt a warm tear softly find its way down my cheek. My usually strong voice quivered as the prayer words came from my mouth and heart.

Deb didn't know that I was sobbing, but God knew.

I could tell I had a new friend for life.

I worked up the courage and then asked boldly, "May I have another appointment with you before we head back to Georgia?"

I held my breath as she quickly answered, "Of course." We looked at her schedule and mine and set up the next visit.

I sauntered out, floating on a God-cloud, wearing a broad smile and singing silently.

The cross of Jesus was before me. The world was behind me. I knew that there was no turning back.

God Chair Journal Entry

Sovereign Lord,
I see the beautiful blue sky but also gray and white clouds overlaying the blue. What are You trying to tell me?

Ann, you can have blue skies galore, and sometimes the blue sky is overlapped by the problems of this world that make you feel a gloomy gray. At that point, Ann, you have a choice to make. You can focus on the gloom or focus forward, looking at Me, your God.

The deceiver aims for you to be a "mess of gloominess" instead of keeping your attention on Me, your Glorious God. Who do you expect will come to Ann's aid?

Truly, it is always You, Lord.

Then Ann, do not allow the cumbersome clouds of gray to sidestep you from seeing Me behind the clouds … I am your calming blue. Gray does not need to conquer you. The blue hue I create is just for you.

CHAPTER 23

Time in the Tundra

Be wise in the way you act toward outsiders;
make the most of every opportunity.
—Colossians 4:5 (NIV)

It was cold when Al and I were in Minnesota. All day. Every day. Did I mention it was December? And we weren't in the South? Each morning, I hopped onto the hotel shuttle, probably weighing ten pounds more than usual. Since this was an everyday occurrence, I'm certain a few people were chuckling. But the slightly overweight snowwoman was ready for anything.

I had read Psalm 91 once again before leaving our hotel room. Verse 11 jumped out at me this day: "For He orders His angels to protect you[, Ann,] wherever you go" (NLT).

Does that mean protection if we get lost again, Lord?

Yes.

How about cold protection?

Yes.

Even if we get some not-so-happy news from a doctor today?

Yes.

The frosty air made my Georgia fingers and toes numb. But the wonderful part of it being so cold outside was that once we arrived at Mayo and peeled off our extra clothing, we didn't have to go outside for the remainder of the day.

The subway. That's how the staff referred to it. Underneath the building was a walking path named the subway. We could go from building to building without going outside, where it was freezing.

The needs of the patient come first. Always. That's one of the many reasons people flocked to Mayo Clinic, I surmised. Every. Single. Person. Cared.

Each Mayo employee was kind, and God knew I needed kindness. He is the best organizer of our lives. He cares. And Mayo cared, meaning less tension for me.

On and on we traveled from one two-hour appointment to the next. When I received the results from the overnight sleep machine, it concurred that I didn't need a full-blown sleep study. Surprise. I knew that.

However, the doctor asked what I did when I woke up in the middle of the night and couldn't go back to sleep.

"Well, after I wrestle with God about why He woke me up and He wins, I place the issues I was ruminating about into His capable hands," I told him confidently.

"God, please handle them so I can rest," I would say in a simple yet desperate-for-rest prayer.

The doctor smiled, agreeing that it was a good idea.

"I like your bracelet," he mentioned, making small talk while walking me back to the waiting room.

Yes, Mayo does that too. Each doctor escorts you back to the waiting room, conversing along the way. Another way to show that the needs of the patient come first.

I glanced at my red rubber "Keep Christ in Christmas" bracelet. It was inexpensive but opened conversations that were priceless, so that's why I felt God wanting me to wear it while in Minnesota.

Smiling, I replied, "I believe that we all need reminders to make the main thing the main thing."

He smiled in return but said nothing more. Planting seeds. I'll know the results in heaven and can rejoice with the angels then. Another gift from Him.

As I headed out to the waiting room to find Al, God brought these words to my mind:

The main thing at Mayo is that the needs of the patient come first. The main thing to God is that the eternal needs of Ann come first.

My spiritual heart was blossoming. My God was teaching me a lot on this Mayo mission trip. God's blessing on me seemed attached to His assignment for me.

We shuttled back to our hotel just in the nick of dark. Still not accustomed to the time change, we hurriedly hopped into bed, my mind thanking Him for the day's events. He is my Sovereign Lord, I remembered, as I relished all that He was up to on this jumbled journey.

No one walks alone at Mayo, even walking back to the waiting room. And with God at my side, I never walk alone through this pilgrimage called life.

Yep. I would come to the tundra again with Him.

And wear two sets of gloves.

And two scarves.

With heavy boots.

Even long johns.

And look like the abominable, weighty snowwoman.

He is magnificently awesome.

And awesome He is.

God Chair Journal Entry

*S*overeign Lord,
I've noticed yellow leaves on our magnolia trees recently. Some are even falling off.

Thank you, Lord, for causing the old foliage in my life to drop so that You can start new growth within me.

Ann, the old in your life that is passing away need not alarm you. The new blooms cannot rise up until the yellow leaves have dropped. I am making a new thing. Watch for the changes.

Thanks to You, Lord, I am ready to come into bloom in a way that I never have blossomed before.

So bring on the lovely new flowers in my life.

The old truly is passing away. The new is bursting forth.

<u>S</u> suddenly
<u>O</u> open to whatever my
<u>A</u> anxious heart had once
<u>R</u> resisted

CHAPTER 24

Morning Has Broken

Praise with elation. Praise every morning.
God's recreation of the new day.
—Eleanor Farjeon, "Morning Has Broken"

I was over-the-moon happy to be at Mayo, yet glad for a short break in the action. Our weekend was calm, quiet, and uneventful, providing a much-needed time away from the daily stress of seemingly endless appointments. My breath yearned for a respite from the weekday pressure. God was gracious and knew that a time of refreshing was vital.

Reading Psalm 91 again, my thoughts went to verse 1: "Those who live in the shelter of the Most High will find rest in the shadow of the Almighty" (NLT).

Why verse 1 again? Rest is what we need this weekend, Lord. Right? No one was asking me questions at Mayo on Saturday or Sunday. Thank You that I can rest in Your sovereignty, not just for the now, but also the forever, Lord.

I again viewed with amazement and joy the turquoise-lighted cross that God lovingly placed in the sky outside our hotel window. He was my faithful Rock of Gibraltar.

My God positioned the cross, as I opened the curtains, to comfort me. I had heard that the color turquoise is associated with serenity, emotional balance, and spiritual grounding. I needed all three.

Eagerly opening those curtains every morning, I saw my colored cross and viewed His glory in it. He was speaking to His little girl from that cross. And in my favorite color, which was icing on the cake.

God is in the tiniest of details. He knew that vibrant color would speak volumes to me. The cross was soothing to my anxious heart. Just like the cross on my knee after my total knee replacement.

I endured frequent cortisone injections for over ten years before I gave in, succumbing to the inevitable surgery. As the incision healed, I noticed the cross scar at the top of my knee. A quite unexpected God-tattoo. I learned that the knee's cruciate ligament derives its name from the Latin word for "cross."

That tiny knee cross is my walking reminder every day. And even fourteen months later, when a staph infection required emergency surgery on that same knee, God kept the cross intact. Our granddaughter said one time, "G.G., I want a cross on my knee."

At breakfast, we saw a woman all alone yet praying before she ate. God opened the door, and I walked through.

"It's nice to see people praying before eating," I said to her as I smiled. "But sad that it's rare." I often use that as an opener when I notice people praying in restaurants.

She slowly opened up, sharing softly that her husband had leukemia so he didn't join her for the meal, due to fasting.

Many of us at the hotel were fasting for bloodwork or waiting for a diagnosis on any given day, which was the norm at hotels in Rochester.

My sister Martha's first husband died of leukemia at age thirty-two.

Life wasn't fair for Martha. Not breathing this long wasn't fair, either. Life is not supposed to be fair, after all. Hard times have sent me prostrate to the foot of the cross.

"For this, we have Jesus." That is what Daddy says a lot, and it's true. My life had been derailed. Would my train ever get on the healthy track again?

I looked at Al's face as he sipped the aromatic coffee, his tense jaw revealing his weariness. I've known this fellow for almost fifty years and can read him well. I clutched his hand, noticing the wrinkles there too. Wisdom wrinkles, I call them. Wrinkles are evidence of a wealth of lessons learned. I had earned my wisdom wrinkles over the years.

The out-loud words nearly stuck in my throat, but I made the effort to force them out. "We are stronger together, Al," I whispered as I leaned closer to him, attempting a confident smile that we both relished. He needed to hear aloud what we both knew was truth: His truth from His throne. Will I see wholeness? That question stuck inside my heart.

Lord, I don't believe in magic, just miracles. Was the first diagnosis true? If not, prepare our hearts for the hard truth. I want to look ahead to a future of health in this life. Am I fooling myself? I don't want to set myself up for a fall. Is it wrong to look ahead of You, Lord, to a fit and vibrant life? You know my desire, but is it Your plan?

I gloried in the reminder that my God was working all of this out for His glory and for my good. When He reminds, He doesn't reprimand. What love.

I attempted to take a deep breath that wouldn't come. For this, I have Jesus.

Magic? No. Miracles? Yes. Al and I were waiting for our miracle to arrive. We were down but not out.

God Chair Journal Entry

Sovereign Lord,

A song from my childhood, from The Bible Songs church songbook, comes to mind. I cut my teeth on songs from the Psalms and am grateful for that spiritual heritage.

"I pray that my words and my thoughts … may all with Thy precepts accord … and ever be pleasing to Thee, my Rock, my Redeemer, my Lord."

Thank You for being my Rock.

"I'm standing on the promises of God."

The foundation for my life is You, my strong Rock.

Thank You are my best Redeemer.

Not only did You redeem me by dying on the cross, but each day, you redeem me from pits I choose to fall into, like a pity party, or the pits that others throw me in that cause great pain to my heart. I recall those words from a Beth Moore Bible study.

Thank You for being my Lord.

Each day, I ask You to be Lord over everything I do: Lord of my choices (that they will be wise choices), Lord of my thoughts (that they will be pure and uplifting), Lord of my steps (that I'll keep my eyes open not to miss any opportunities You place on my path).

For

You are my strongest Rock,

You are my best Redeemer,

You are my kindest Lord, and I thank You.

Ann, thank you for remembering to thank Me. I hold onto you firmly, never letting you go. I turn you in the direction of My choosing and bend you to walk in the way I would have you to go.

CHAPTER 25

Functional Breathing Whatchamacallit

Why do I feel so confused? So many different emotions.
Am I happy? Scared? Excited? Nervous?
—Mary Katherine Gainey, *Ecuador*

Sure enough, I awoke to another day at Mayo. Up and at 'em, Ann. Put your smile on. I do believe that my Mighty God will make me live again, breathe again to live again. Clinging to that optimistic desire, a part of me wondered, would He really put breath back into me? I knew He could because He was able. But would He? Was that His best plan for me?

Functional breathing disorder, triggered by that simple procedure, is what the general internist said to us. I pondered, "What do these words mean separately, spiritually?" Curious, and having time between appointments, I grabbed my phone dictionary.

"A functional disorder: When an organ doesn't work as it should." I rolled my eyes. Tell me something I don't know. I read on.

"A functional breathing disorder: when lungs don't work as they should."

Got it. Simple. Kindergarten level. But what are You trying to teach me, Lord? I'm yearning to learn. Separating each word might help.

Functional

- having a special task
  I believe, Lord, that You are refining me for my next assignment, but the process stinks, just so You know.
- intended to be used
  God, Your plan is to use me, to give me a future and a hope, as Jeremiah 29:11 reminds me so clearly. Can you use a nonbreather, if that is what You ordain for the rest of my life? That means no healing.
- capable of functioning
  Lord, I can only function well when I cling well. This journey is forcing me to grab on to You as never before. But my arms are dog-tired from holding on doggedly to the hem of Your garment. And where is Aaron to lift the tired arms of Moses?
- serving a purpose for which it was designed
  The Westminster Shorter Catechism, etched in my mind from youth, reminds me that "Man's [Ann's] chief end is to glorify God and to enjoy Him forever." So my purpose is to glorify You with my life, Lord, and to enjoy You forever. I can do that through sharing this journey with others. But I wonder if I'll be too worn out to tell others what I'm learning through the pain? And when will there be gain?

Breathing

- to take rest
  Lord, You have slowed me down for certain. I am pushing on, but it's an uphill battle.
- to pause, as for breath
  I am learning to pause before Your throne to gather Your breath into my lungs. I want Your breath to replace my breath. Yet, when?
- inhale/exhale
  God, as I inhale more of You, I can exhale You to a hurting world. Inhaling and exhaling is my desire, but I'm not handling inhaling well, as You know.
- to take oxygen in
  I can't survive without You giving me oxygen, the breath of life. Will these bones ever rejoice?

- respiration/a single breath
  Lord, this health voyage is teaching me that You alone give me every precious breath as a gift. I promise to use the gift wisely, Sir, if it's ever to happen. After all, it's been over two years so far. What do I have to show for the wait but a pile of ever-mounting medical bills and emotional pain?

Disorder

- a state of confusion
  Well, Lord, enough said. I still remain confused as to how You will use this. But I am trusting because You are not the author of confusion.
- to disturb the regular function
  God, have You disturbed "regular Ann" to make a "better Ann," perhaps? I'm disturbed and would like a confirmation.
- to disrupt the neat arrangement
  My life was neat, tidy, and well-managed until You turned my breathing world topsy-turvy. Was that the plan for Ann? For just a season? Forever? Or until I learned my lessons well? I recall those lyrics. Our daughter enjoyed being part of the Godspell *musical while a student at Erskine College, my alma mater.*
- a breach of the peace or public order
  Can there be peace in the murky misery? There is always peace in Your presence, but sometimes it seems so far off in the distance that I struggle to grasp it.

I read synonyms like "messy," "chaos," "complication," "malady," "trouble," "infirmity," and "ailment." I felt all of those emotions.

Stop already. No more. I get it. Sickness is sickening.

A friend reminded me over lunch that God doesn't always answer our prayers the way we expect. But He will give us a godly answer that we may not like one little bit. I couldn't have said it better.

So yes and no. Yes, I was thrilled to have a name for this nonmelodious malady. No, I wasn't thrilled with the lengthy time it would take to get well, if I were to heal.

As I said to one Mayo doc, "I was hoping to take one purple pill, be done with it, and go on with my life."

He smiled because we both knew better. And what verse jumped from my Bible in the hotel room this morning from Psalm 91? Verse 2, naturally. Father knows best.

"This I declare of the Lord: He alone is my refuge, my place of safety; He is my God and I trust Him" (NLT).

Another day at Mayo. Of living. Of learning. Of sometimes still just trying to survive with Him at the helm.

As I plopped into bed that night, I heard Annie (from the musical *Annie*) singing in the background. Would the sun come out tomorrow?

Goodnight, Annie.

Goodnight, God, who created Little Annie Rooney.

Daddy called me that when I was quite small. It was from the comic strip that he read in the newspaper. Although it was a simple jingle from the popular song of the early 1900s, I felt special each time he got on his knees, down to my short level, looked into my eyes, smiled only at me, and sang the line "Little Annie Rooney is my sweetheart." Even though I'm a big girl now, sometimes I'm just a confused little girl. Little and weak, but strong in Him. Little Annie Rooney will live to tell of His greatness.

Another friend often says that "little is much with God in it." Remember that, Little Annie Rooney.

God Chair Journal Entry

Sovereign Lord,
I did have sweet tea with caffeine for lunch. Please settle me down, so that I can relax in our time together.

Ann, you are My vessel. Look at that empty flowerpot (vessel) on the deck. I take the unhealthy patterns (unhealthy breathing, unhealthy emotional issues, unhealthy spiritual issues) out of your body (vessel) to fill your life (vessel) with My breath within you, My strength within you, My confidence within you, and My joy within you.

Look at the birds that I caused to fly through the trees off the deck just now. Was the blue one a beautiful creation of Mine? Of course. If I care for the birds of the air so wonderfully, you can trust that I'll always care for you.

Lord, what was significant about You choosing a blue bird to cross my path and not a red or a brown one?

Ann, blue is a calming color. I wanted to soothe your mind to remind you of My soothing and calming care over you constantly.

Lord, I will slow down and shift my perspective.
I will breathe in You.
I will.

CHAPTER 26

Won't Someone Ask Me?

The Lord is not slow in keeping His promise,
as some understand slowness.
—2 Peter 3:9a (NIV)

As usual, I began another Mayo day reading Psalm 91 in our hotel room. First thing. There was a great deal on my plate. His words were helpful and calming to me as I began another long day overflowing with appointments.

Verse 3 pranced off the page this morning: "For He will rescue you[, Ann,] from every trap and protect you from the fatal plague" (NLT).

Yes, Lord. Rescue me. Protect me. And, by the way, is this breathing issue a trap from the deceiver or a fatal plague? Or perhaps a blessing in disguise? Who knew? He knew, but He wasn't talking, yet.

Little did I know that the high point of this particular day would be words straight from His throne to my heart. I had no clue when I awoke that morning. God was about to bless me indeed, and it was to be His surprise just for His little lass.

I wanted someone at Mayo to ask me how I had been surviving with this type of shallow breathing for two and a half years. At home, I had prayed that request and shared my desire with Al before we left on this trip.

Today's schedule revealed that I was to see a fibromyalgia/chronic fatigue specialist, and I wasn't pleased. I don't need this specialist. I just need to breathe. What are these Mayo people thinking? What is God thinking? I was ranting and raving to myself.

As it turned out, God knew exactly what I needed this day: a specialist I thought I didn't need.

In the waiting room, I had to fill out thirty (or was it three hundred?) pages. I would pay mightily for someone to complete all of this for me. Diagrams of the body. Put an X where you hurt.

You people. I don't hurt. I can't breathe. Why is no one listening? So by the time I sat down in the exam room, I was fit to be tied. When the doctor came in, I tried to conceal my anger, lecturing myself to remain tranquil.

"I guess you want me to share my story," I said, attempting a smile and hoping to hide my frustration.

"Nope," he said. "I read all the reports last night from the other doctors you've seen here so far."

That's how this diagnostic team approach works at Mayo. After each doctor saw me, a report was sent online. I could read it, as well as each of the doctors who had seen me. This new doctor got my attention immediately.

"When you had the medical trauma in 2015, your body interpreted it like a nuclear event, as if a bomb had exploded inside of your brain." He paused long enough for my mind to hop into his illustration.

Yes. Exactly. How did he know?

He continued, "So the question I have for you is, how have you been breathing like this for years?"

My eyes grew large. I leaned over, sat up straight, and pointed an arthritic finger as I excitedly blurted out these now memorable words: "You are the answer to my prayer." I then told him what I had prayed.

He was good at stories, so he shared his own. His back surgery had caused the same result. After his surgery, he had back pain when there was no pain to be had. But it was real to his body because his brain had told his body incorrect information. It was clear that he understood my situation.

"That means so much to me. I'm not making this up. I'm not looney or a hypochondriac."

He smiled, having had those thoughts about himself.

"This is real, Ann." He called it real. He believed me. Encouraged by his words, I continued sharing my own illustration.

"I feel as if I've been treading water in a deep lake. At first, my arms and legs were strong, so it was easy to stay afloat. But after so long a time, my once-vigilant extremities are worn out. It has been almost impossible to keep my head above water, physically and emotionally. With each passing day, I have become increasingly disillusioned. I might drown. In fact, I am almost certain of it."

Just speaking those words showed me that my feelings were becoming unmanageable. Once resilient, I was fading fast.

"Ann, you have been spiraling down for over two years, and we don't want you to go down any lower. You are at Mayo now, and you won't drown."

Vividly, he added a word picture: "But the castle will have to be broken down first before you can rebuild your life."

It was amazing how talking cleared the air.

Right away, I could visualize my castle; I wanted my castle back. Yearning to be complete again, I had hope.

He looked at my sheet of appointments for the day, revealing a fibromyalgia/chronic fatigue educational class next, lasting several hours.

"You don't need that session," he said with confidence, chuckling. "That's not your issue, so there's no need to waste your time."

I couldn't have said it better myself, I thought, beaming with relief.

He grabbed a blank sheet of paper to draw a diagram. I was silent as I watched the line plummet near the bottom of the page. "Here you are. You came to Mayo, thinking you were already at the bottom, but you aren't. But if you hadn't come here, you know what the bottom would have been." He paused to look deeply into my eyes, watching for a facial reaction. I didn't want to say the words aloud.

Yet, I did know. Heaven with Mama. In the stillness of his steely eyes, I immediately knew what he was conveying.

"But you are going to be fine. Really, you are."

That was reassuring. I almost breathed a deep sigh of happiness, if I could have breathed deeply.

As Al and I left his office, I had a silent conversation. *I'm beginning to believe I'll be fine.*

Really.

God Chair Journal Entry

Sovereign Lord,
I like the sunshine, but … I love the Son-shine.

God, You are so cool. You are
C coordinating the
O opening of
O opportunities for
L life in eternity with You.

Thank You for giving me opportunities each day to brag on You to a hurting world because I yearn to see more people spend eternity with You and me.

(tune of "Are You Sleeping," my version)
Are you listening?
Are you listening?
Little Ann? Little Ann?
I am speaking to you.
I am speaking to you.
Hear it now.
Heed My plan.

You give me the coolest songs, Lord.

Ann, I am the creator of melodies, especially the melodies of your life.

CHAPTER 27

Deer in the Headlights

Slip slidin' away. Slip slidin' away. You know the nearer
your destination, the more you're slip slidin' away.
—Paul Simon, "Slip Slidin' Away"

Oh, dear. It's a deer. And I'm not in a forest.

A friend of mine posted a video on YouTube of an Oregon firefighter steering a deer, hoping to guide it across an ice-covered lake to safety on the shore.[2] The problem was that the deer's head was turned away from the land.

As I watched the video while at Mayo, I saw myself as the deer, lost on the frozen lake, not knowing how close I was to the security of land, shaking for dear life.

I saw Mayo Clinic as the raft and God as the firefighter, nudging my face ever so gently. By turning around, I could visualize the safety in His plan to guide me when I couldn't see the forest for the trees.

Where was He guiding me? I had no idea. Healing? That was my prayer and the prayer of those lifting me up before His throne. Safety? Always in Him. But there was a fearful side of me at Mayo. Being so tired, I was skeptical. Could I make it to safety? The deer wasn't certain either because he couldn't see the shore.

I wasn't Peter walking on water. I was Ann sliding across ice: a mere human who was seriously scared.

I showed the YouTube video to my Mind Body Medicine counselor, and it resonated with her too. Her eyes opened wide, just like the deer and exactly like mine. We became "dear, deer" friends in an instant. Every time I send her a text, it ends with "your 'deer' friend." And she replies with the same.

The deer was floundering when rescue was so near. Is that what I was doing? Floundering? Is rescue really near? Could I even hope to be set free? Like the deer, I was too fearful to believe that healing just might be on earth.

I am weak in the knees, Lord, like that deer on the icy pond. I can see his lanky legs trembling, as were mine. Will I ever be healthy again? Dare I hope so? I'm praying so.

Was God lovingly turning my hesitant head, showing me that the healing shore was close and within my reach? Maybe right in front of me?

The firefighter gently focused the anxious deer's head toward land. The human saw that safety was in reach, but did the deer? Not so much. Different perspectives and vantage points.

Is safety and healing within my reach, Lord? Am I scared to death? Or perhaps pointed toward life?

My vision is blurry, so I can't see the truth, much less the shoreline. What is His strategy for me?

Nor can I see the light at the end of the tunnel. Does the tunnel even have an ending? If it does, why isn't it visible?

Make it real, Lord. Could I heal, Lord? I'm still a frightened deer, wondering if life will ever be the same again.

Mayo Clinic is great. But God is greater.

What will be the outcome for Ann? Frightened Ann. Little Annie Rooney. Raggedy Ann. "Deer" me.

I'm tired of being on the ice, slip slidin' away. Is there relief in sight? Is there land, possibly a shore of safety for me?

Or is Ann to be no more?

I'd roll the dice, but I'm not a gambler. Remember to trust, Ann. I am too fragile to trust. Yet perhaps I'm too spent to do anything but trust.

T Timidly

R relying

U upward to

S stand

T tall in His strength.

God gave me that acronym when our son had his near-death truck accident. Those words comforted many others in their time of need. I can trust Him even with this long struggle.

Maybe I can be brave and stand up, even with wobbly legs, like the deer. After all, God is my firefighter. He led me to shore during a variety of tough times in the past.

Can I really stand tall in His strength, though timidly?

Time will tell.

The shore is there.

God has turned my head to see it.

Will I make it to safety and healing?

How can I be sure?

I'm not a deer, after all.

And my legs are shaky.

Oh, dear.

God Chair Journal Entry

Sovereign Lord,
You kept me going when I didn't have a diagnosis.
I was scared. You were not.
I was confused. You were not.
I was weary. You were not.
I was wondering. You were not.
I was clueless. You were not.
I was weak. You were not.
I was disheartened. You were not.
I was anxious. You were not.
I was tense. You were not.
I was surprised. You were not.
I was vulnerable. You were not.
I was a mess. You were not.

Ann, You can't survive well without Me. You can stumble without Me, sink to the bottom without Me, make a mess of things without Me, and struggle without Me. But You can't run away without Me, for I always follow you. Relentlessly. Even in hard places, I am there. Ann, I am there when you stumble, sink, try to do it alone, make a mess, struggle, and most of all, when you think you are running away.

Lord, I'll always follow You to the end.

CHAPTER 28

Ann's Avalanche

And they all go marching down to the ground to get
out of the rain. Boom! Boom! Boom! Boom!
—Robert D. Singleton, "The Ants Go Marching"

Avalanche. Why did that word come to my mind? I squelched a giggle
that morning while getting ready for another day filled with Mayo
appointments.

Curious, I turned to the dictionary to find a deeper meaning: "a
sudden arrival or occurrence of something in overwhelming quantities."

Curious no more, I really laughed (glad Al was in the shower).
Avalanche is right on with what I'm feeling. That's it. I am in an appointment
avalanche.

After dressing for yet another frigid day, I read Psalm 91 again. What
jumped out at me, probably because of the avalanche connection, were
verses 9 and 10.

"If you, [Ann], make the Lord your refuge, if you make the Most High
your shelter, [Ann], no evil will conquer you; no plague will come near
your dwelling" (NLT).

God, You are indeed my refuge and my shelter. No plague can harm
me. No avalanche of appointments will overwhelm me.

After all, God brought me to Mayo. On a mission. Well, two, in fact.
A mission to get a diagnosis, and a mission of being used, as God was
stretching me along the way.

You are so efficient. Grinning like a Cheshire cat, I looked heavenward to see if I could catch His smile. I was confident that I saw it.

Shallow breathing surely makes these appointments more strenuous. I thought of yesterday's appointment avalanche.

Blood drawn. Basement.

Pulmonary consultation: fifteenth floor (or was that seventeenth)?

Breathing class. Got lost. Staff helped.

Follow up with Internal Medicine to discuss lab results.

Shuttled over to the Mayo Clinic Hospital, St. Marys Campus. Looked lost. Was lost. Helped again by their staff.

Each day was like that. I was tense and tired. And getting more tense and more tired by the day. Then there was homework, in the evening, when I had no sparkle left.

Watch a CD on central sensitization. Not once. Three times. Tonight? Three whole times? Really? Don't they know I'm up to my ears with processing new information? I was in a daily avalanche of learning new terms.

"Explain that once more," I kept saying to each medical person; some appointments took close to two hours. They were exceedingly patient.

Exhaustion was setting in. I could feel the weight, so the hotel room became our haven, safe from the avalanche.

My sweet husband found funny movies on his laptop for us to watch. He was trying to keep me uplifted. *I'm keeping him,* I mused.

God, You won't let the avalanche overtake me. You have sent me on a Mayo ministry mission. I was convinced. Thinking about the joy of the mission always lifted me from exhaustion to invigoration. No missed opportunities.

I heard years ago that it takes people an average of seven times of hearing the gospel before they ask Jesus into their heart. My job is to be obedient and share Him with those He placed on my path.

I had used that illustration when I trained new volunteer patient advocates at Choices Pregnancy Care Center. For twenty-five years, we shared His truth, but God touches hearts. I can see me now, the teacher. I would tell the ladies that if a patient prays to receive Christ, just realize that you could be that seventh person.

"And if they don't, what then?" There was always one overly eager trainee.

If they don't ask Christ into their heart, just remember that you were the fourth person. That way, I would conclude, you can't be boastful or feel as if you didn't do a good enough job. What a restful, freeing place to be.

And God yearns for us to be free in Him.

My only job description is to brag on Him. Period. He sends His Holy Spirit to do the heart work. Period.

After hanging up my clothes and taking a much-needed warm shower, I lay down to rest my worn to a frazzle bones and tense muscles following another exhausting day of appointments galore.

My thoughts were comforting, for the Master of my soul assured me that the appointment avalanche wouldn't be my demise. I stared at the ceiling but really up at Him.

I am nothing. How freeing.

You are everything. How comforting.

I'll keep on marching, just like the ants in the children's song that I learned in my youth from Aunt Glynn, sang with our children, and taught the grandchildren.

Resting in that remembrance, I could feel myself starting to drift off. Safe sleep. Sacred sleep.

But I wasn't counting sheep nor the doctor sheep as before.

I was watching the ants go marching, one by one. Zzzz.

God Chair Journal Entry

Sovereign Lord,
I am closing my eyes and hearing a bird utter three tweets and then pausing, then the same three tweets and pausing again.

I am hearing You tell me the bird is saying, "Praise Me now, praise Me now, praise Me now."

So, Lord of my life, here I go:
I praise You for Your goodness, for Your might, for Your majesty, for loving me despite me, for the comfort You send me through the Holy Spirit, for letting me take a few deep breaths of this breeze blowing through my hair.

I am here in Your presence, Lord.
Speak to me. I am listening.
Fill me with Your breath. I wait.

Ann, I have redeemed you to use you. My love inside you allows you, then, to love others well. My love lifts you up so that you can, then, lift others up. Keep watching for your assignments each day.

Yes, Sir. I'm honored to do so.

CHAPTER 29

Mama Look-Alike

Now when times come where my thoughts get tangled, dark and
clang, I will recall her sermons in song. And thank God she sang.
—Martha B. Morgan, *Mama*

I awoke in a bittersweet mood. It was my last day of Mayo appointments,
yet my glad frame of mind was sad as well.

I had a confirmed diagnosis. Glad.

I had made new friends. Glad.

I had to leave new friends. Sad.

Especially my favorite, Deb. Sadder.

But no thinking about that now. First things first. Put on the entire
snowwoman garb, Ann, and don't forget to read Psalm 91. Ahh. That will
make me smile.

Verse 14: "The Lord says, 'I will rescue those who love Me. I will
protect those who trust in My name'" (NLT).

You have rescued me. You have protected me. I have trusted You.
There were only a few appointments today. It was my last day, after all.
Everything was culminating to an end. Winding down yet pointing to a
beginning as well.

I was thrilled to be able to see my favorite Mayo person for a second
time. All she can say is no, I thought, as I bravely asked, "May I see you
once more before I leave?"

"Surely," she smiled, penciling me in.

The appointment was to be the last day. This day. I had been waiting with bated breath. Checking my watch in excitement. Now it was time, yet I wondered how it would unfold. Al was with me, as he was for most appointments. As before, he took his place by my side, with his paper and pen. That comfort never got old.

She and I were facing one another. My new friend. All of a sudden, as she was talking, I saw Mama's ears. Then I noticed her forehead. I saw Mama's forehead. Her hair color and texture. Mama's hair. What was happening?

As I looked intently at her entire face, I began to see my mama. A quite younger version but the way I remembered Mama at this woman's age. Why did I not see this before, at the first appointment? I had been with her for two hours. God didn't reveal it before, but He did now.

This was wonderfully strange. Only God possesses such wonderful strangeness in His gifts to His children.

Mama had been in heaven for years, yet God sent her to Mayo. For her little girl. Her eldest.

At the end of our session, I asked to pray. As at that first appointment, my voice cracked. Like clockwork, a tear trickled down my cheek as I uttered the prayer. Mama was here.

God was faithful to Sydney Ann Beckham Gainey, once again.

As she walked us out to the waiting room, I explained what had just happened in her office. About sensing Mama in her face.

My voice quaked.

My chin quivered.

But I got the words out.

It was important for me to verbalize God's powerfully wonderful gift. He loved me that much.

We hugged. I knew we would. What I wasn't expecting was to feel Mama's arms, yet I did. Another strangely wonderful experience. I didn't want to let go of Deb because I would be sending Mama back to heaven. Reluctantly, I released our embrace. Mama was gone.

When we left, Al said that he, having the side view of her face, had thought during the appointment, that she looked like Uncle Grady, Mama's baby brother. They do look similar. More so as they had aged. Confirmation.

Both Al and I had seen Mama. I wasn't crazy, or perhaps we both were. God, how do You always know what I need even when I don't know what I need? He smiled, knowing that was a silly question. I was floating on a blissful cloud but deferred to walking out instead of doing a Jesus dance in front of those we passed in the waiting room. I could save dancing before Him for our hotel room.

What a best day ever at Mayo. I pondered the ten days, filled with the marvelous grace of God, as I slipped under the covers. The last night in our hotel home. The delightful day's events had hyped me up, and I was attempting to unwind by thinking, reflecting on the day and on Mama's hug.

Martha had written a poem about Mama that she read at the memorial service many years ago. I had not memorized it but wanted to retrieve the words for such a time as this.

Straining my brain to recall, I asked God for just one line. Then, out of the blue, it came straight from His throne to my heart: "She sang 'Trust and Obey' as the way to deal with strife."

That was what I needed to hear. My journey wasn't over yet. The next step was the treatment plan. Was I up to walking the next path?

Ann, remember Mama's words. Trust. Obey. Those words will serve you well as you move forward.

Was I saying that to myself, or was God telling me? Perhaps Mama was speaking, looking down from heaven as she watched her firstborn.

Mary Katherine had given me a picture frame years back that stays on my nightstand. The two of us are in the picture, sitting on the steps of a log cabin. I recalled the words written at the bottom of the frame: "It's strange when you realize you are starting to sound like your mother and it makes sense."

That is truth, I thought. It didn't matter who was saying it to me. It was truth.

Trust. Obey. His Truth.

So as not to wake Al, I silently continued the song with the line, "There's no other way."

Now that was Mama. I could hear her singing, "to be happy in Jesus, but to trust and obey."

I can almost see her.

Her hands, not on her hips, but outstretched.
Smiling at her little one.
The eldest.
You're right, Mama.
I will trust Him. I will obey Him.
Because there's no other way.

God Chair Journal Entry

Sovereign Lord,
What blessings You have bestowed on me:

- blessings that immediately felt like blessings
- blessings that took time to see them as blessings

Ann, you are now seeing little blessings since I have slowed you down by blessing you with this breathing issue. You are noticing the breeze, a bird's special tweet, the clouds I move across the sky, and oh, so much more. You are noticing Me more, which is the best blessing.

Yes, Lord. Being stopped in my tracks on August 6, 2015, has sent me "blessings upon blessings" from You.

Pain with purpose, Lord. You are the giver of every good and perfect gift.

Lord, I remember from school that heat, pressure, along with time, make diamonds. Are you developing an Ann-diamond? If so, I suppose that right now, I am a diamond in the rough.

Ann, You can rest assured that I am the Diamond-Maker. Just watch Me work. Stay tuned.

CHAPTER 30

Marvelous Mayo

Jesus, take the wheel.
Take it from my hands.
'Cause I can't do this on my own.
I'm letting go.
—Brett James, Hillary Lindsey, Gordon
Sampon, "Jesus, Take the Wheel"

The diagnosis arrived on the doorstep of my heart. I woke up, thinking it was another day at Mayo. It made sense. After all, we had been here for almost two weeks.

Wait. There were no more appointments. But I had my marching orders in hand and was ready to start.

The end of Mayo.

The beginning of the treatment plan.

I had listened intently, but it was also written on the paper the staff gave me, just in case my memory failed. Reading it again, I felt overwhelmed.

- physical therapy: three times a week for twelve weeks
- counseling and trauma work
- cognitive behavioral therapy to retrain my brain
- yoga, to aid in returning to normal breathing
- acupuncture, to regulate breathing
- deep tissue massage, relieving tension while creating calmness

Each doctor had hypothesized a different length of time it could take to recover. They didn't know. Only God did.

I heard

- "Perhaps a month" (the encourager),
- "Maybe six months or longer" (the realist), and
- "You may never completely heal" (the truth?).

While still in Minnesota, Al and I decided that I would use my former physical therapist, who was also a friend of my husband's; I called immediately to make my first appointment for the following Monday. Let's get this show on the road.

Having already accomplished part of this plan, by setting up the first physical therapy appointment, I probably looked puffed up. But I had to be confident, right?

I think I can. I think I can.

Stop, Ann.

I know I will. I know I will.

I could do this. I would do this. There were no problems. All I had in my hand were solutions, and I felt ready and raring to begin. That had to be my thought pattern. Focused. Remember the Bible verse, Ann. You can do anything in His strength.

But what if I can't do it all? What if total healing doesn't happen, Lord? I don't want to live in La-La Land, so I must be a realist. Deep breath, I thought, wishing I could actually take one.

"Ann believes. Help Ann's unbelief," I whispered to God's throne of grace.

Jesus, take the wheel. I'm letting go. And letting You.

That's when the airplane pilot broke in on my God-thought. I grabbed Al's hand and looked into his eyes for support. I had a feeling that we needed God to show up big time as we progressed toward the next segment of this breathing trip.

"Welcome aboard. We expect a smooth flight."

As I listened to the pilot's voice, I heard God even louder through His heavenly megaphone: "Ann, welcome aboard the treatment plan. There may be some turbulence ahead."

What did that mean? I nervously contemplated all possibilities; some sounded promising, others not so much.

Then I distinctly and confidently heard Mama add, with outstretched hands, "Eldest of mine, just trust and obey."

I promise that I will, Mama.

God Chair Journal Entry

Sovereign Lord,
Why does my body ache?

Ann, it's because of your "achy, breaky heart," and I can heal your heart. Healing hearts has always been My specialty.

Well, Lord, I am ready to be healed of this breathing debility.
I am willing for You to heal me in every area that needs healing: spiritually, physically, emotionally, mentally.

I am ready, I'm willing, You are able.
I rest in You for each step along the way.

Ann, in Me, you can be strong, you can be confident, you can be fearless, you can be trusting, you can be courageous, and most of all, you can be God-controlled.

Lord,
I came to this chair.
I saw You.
I conquered myself.
I came. I saw. I conquered.
What rest.

CHAPTER 31

The Sunny South Flight

For we are God's handiwork, created in Christ Jesus to do good
works, which God prepared in advance for us [and Ann] to do.
—Ephesians 2:10 (NIV)

We were leaving the cold of Minnesota and taking with us the warmth
of the God-ordained people we had met. Bittersweet, indeed. I smiled a
sigh, rejoicing in the memorable God-experiences at Mayo Clinic. People
say that home is where the heart is. It would be good to get back to
Georgia, but I knew I had left a part of my heart, not in San Francisco,
but Minnesota.

After getting settled on the airplane, I had a conversation with God.
"Going home seems anticlimactic, Sir."

"Ann, your journey has just begun."

Reality seized me. Bigger fish to fry. Counselors to find. A yoga class
to locate. Acupuncture and massage appointments to find their places on
the calendar. And Christmas was ten days away.

"Lord, would you consider moving Christmas to late January, just
this once?"

I attempted some reading on the flight back but wasn't able to focus
well. The ten-day trip had caught up with both of us. But I didn't nap,
as I don't sleep sitting up, but my other half is quite capable of that feat.
Glancing at Al's head, I saw it starting to collapse onto my shoulder.

He had shouldered my breathing issue for so very long. I suppose it's only right for me to shoulder his head on this flight. It's the least I can do, right, God?

In the frantic hustle and bustle of packing up, leaving the hotel, and getting to the airport, it dawned on me that I had not yet read Psalm 91 that day. After settling down in my seat, I searched my book bag and finally pulled it out.

The Bible was my go-to airplane reading. Always. As I finished the chapter, the last two verses jumped onto my shoulder, but I moved them to my lap so Al's head could rest. This trip had taken a toll on him too.

I read verse 15: "When they [Al and Ann] call on Me, I will answer; I will be with them in trouble. I will rescue them and honor them" (NLT).

Meditating on the verse, I acknowledged God by looking at His infinite sky and said to my Master, *Of course You answer. You gave me a diagnosis. The treatment plan is in hand. I'll work the plan, Sir. Fast and furiously. You know the Ann You created. Thy will be done. Yet You mention trouble in verse 15; what kind of trouble could there be now?*

I gazed intensely at the sky; it looked as immense as my many questions.

I didn't sense an answer from Him, even though I was listening. Perhaps He wanted to shield me from envisioning the serious storm that the treatment plan would unveil all too soon.

Lord, the verse mentions rescue and honor. I don't need rescuing anymore. Absolutely I don't. Or do I?

He didn't respond to that question, either. *Hmmm. That causes me to wonder what could be up ahead, Lord. If there is ensuing trouble on the horizon, You will rescue me and honor me. That is what You say in Your Word. I can rest in the confidence of Your sovereignty.*

But it was all so elusive, this treatment plan. I glanced out the window at the clouds and felt His presence among them. What a heavenly feeling, being so close to heaven.

I'll rest in You, Lord.

He lovingly replied, "Rest and relax, Ann."

Whatever trouble may lie before me, God and I are a team. Along with Al. Together. Somehow.

Verse 16 came next: "I will satisfy them [Al and Ann] with a long life and give them My salvation."

A long life. That sounds satisfying, as well as gratifying. But salvation?

I already have that, Lord. I know that I'll spend eternity in heaven, saved from eternal separation from You. Are You to save me from the length of the treatment plan too? Or promise to be with me through it?

I believe there is redemption ahead of me from this functional breathing disorder. Is God going to teach me even more during the next step of this health journey? Will what I learn not be just for Ann? For my family and friends, perhaps? A widening circle, even? Those who don't know me? Some who will never meet me this side of heaven? These questions were floating around through my brain and out the airplane windows.

God's ways often seem convoluted and confusing yet perfectly sensible at the same time. I knew that every Christ-follower had a story, which is His story about our story.

Was God revealing that I was going to write a book about this experience? Surely not. Writing is too hard. But wait. The woman at Mayo had said there was a book in me. And so had Al. For years now. How could they know? I have never written a book. I don't know how to write a book. God knew that. Would He take me out of my comfort zone again?

Glancing at the fluffy clouds outside the airplane window, I wondered. A lot. Little did I know how many treacherous months of working the plan it would take for healing to be a reality. An airplane couldn't take me there fast. Walking this painful path had been like a slow boat to China already, and it wasn't over yet. Imagining what this upcoming walk would entail felt overwhelming. And I was already worn to a frazzle. I looked at Al. He was exhausted, too, but sleeping. I was glad that he was resting. But why can't I sleep on an airplane, Sovereign Boss of Ann? Then His whisper came (or maybe it was Mama's):

Trust. Obey.

Before I knew it, the airplane wheels came down, slamming us to an abrupt halt. As we gathered our luggage, I talked with my Maker.

Lord, You parted the Red Sea so that I could walk right through it to Mayo Clinic. What is next? I asked that in a timid but trusting-to-be-healed way.

Then the words to that old hymn resonated in my spirit: "No turning back. No turning back." True. I wouldn't turn back. Forging ahead is the only way forward to good health.

We stepped out of the airplane and into the world's busiest airport,

Hartsfield-Jackson Atlanta International Airport. We were close to home now.

Another long walk was ahead of us to get outside into the open air. I tried not to get ahead of myself with eagerness, knowing that we weren't home yet.

After loading all our luggage from the entire ten-day trip into the small rental car, we settled in for the hour drive in the dark to home sweet home, relieved to be on the last leg of our trip, but not eager to sit again.

I positioned my tired body into the passenger seat, wondering if just maybe I could nap. That was laughable; it would be a first for me.

As the car engine revved up, I turned my heavy head to look at Al, glad that one of us had gotten some rest.

God Chair Journal Entry

Sovereign Lord,
The clouds are floating by. They look like sticky, moving cotton candy.

May I never do anything but stick to You, Lord, like cotton candy sticks together.

I just noticed a wasp building a nest in the clear enclosed outlet on the deck. That insect has no idea that the nest can't get much bigger because of the cover surrounding it.

Lord, forgive me for unknowingly setting my sights so small. May I see You for the huge God that You are, ever wanting to do more than I can ask.

You are doing a new thing in me, making Ann newer and better than before. It's about to spring forth.

The Prayer of Jabez found in 1 Chronicles 4:10 (NKJV) (with my additions):
Oh, that You would bless me indeed [more and more]
And enlarge my territory [not living in a covered deck outlet]
That Your hand would be with me [I can't do anything without You]
And that You would keep me from evil [I trust Your protection]
That I may not cause pain (to others or myself].

THE TASK

CHAPTER 32

Working the Plan

I know what to say. It's the sayin' of it.
—The Little Minister (1934)

Home was a sight for sore eyes. Elliott and Jessica had left a basket of goodies on the foyer floor with a "Happy Diagnosis Day" note. After having my diagnosis confirmed by the Mayo team, Al and I were eager to get into bed and fluff our own pillows. I yearned for the rest of the journey to be over, but that wasn't going to happen. The treatment plan that lay before me seemed like a nine-foot-tall Goliath. Little did I know that the hard work ahead would be the equivalent of a television show, in living color, played out before my very eyes. How long would it take to get well? That was what I didn't know yet wished I did.

Well, Mayo didn't know, either. The last doctor said, "You may never completely heal."

My mouth didn't reveal what my heart was screaming: *I don't receive that,* I silently yelled while wearing a smile like curly-haired redhead Annie would. I felt in my innermost being that God was going to heal me, totally.

Rejecting that one doctor's comment, I felt confident that he hadn't meant to discourage me. Giving me the worst-case scenario just made me stronger. Perhaps that's why God allowed him to say those hard-to-hear words. Life could be messy at times.

One thing was certain: No one could travel this road with me. I was the one who would walk circles around myself on this healing walk. My fix-it husband couldn't do it for me. If Al thought he could have, he would have.

So it was just me. Okay then. I checked to see that the blinders were on tightly to do that rough-and-tumble work, to being healed 100 percent, by God's grace.

Heal and be revealed. I said that brief but powerful prayer often when standing in the gap for others.

- When I heard a siren:
  "Lord, heal and be revealed."
- When I passed a fire truck:
  "Lord, heal and be revealed."
- When I didn't know what words to pray for someone:
  "Lord, heal and be revealed."

"So, Lord, heal me through this time of purposeful therapeutic work. And be revealed to me in ways I've never experienced, until now."

My treatment plan was clear. The marching orders were detailed on paper, and my first physical therapy appointment was right around the corner. This particular physical therapist had been part of my healing plan twice before, so that helped. He had worked with me through my first knee replacement and then, fourteen months later, when I had a staph infection in the same knee, requiring emergency surgery, a PICC line, and antibiotics through that tube every eight hours for six weeks. We had a common ground of living a Christ-directed life, which was a plus.

God, please heal and be revealed, in all of this healing hoopla called the treatment plan, daunting though it appears. God, are You to teach me patience through all of this?

What I didn't know was how strenuous this specific type of physical therapy would be. It was different from therapy on my knee. Sometimes, tough issues are approached easier as surprises. That way, you don't overthink or second-guess. *Do not overthink, Ann. Or second-guess. Be strong in the Lord.*

"This is the day that the Lord has made. I won't dread anything in it" (my translation of Psalm 118:24).

I will not dread anything.

I will not dread.

I will not.

I won't dread what tomorrow may bring. Put on courage. My heart was beating courage, but my breath breathed tension.

God Chair Journal Entry

Sovereign Lord,
What a very windy day. The trees, as well as I, seem weak and bent over from the biting wind. We are both hanging on for dear life.

Ann, you always have a choice. You can choose to see the world or to see Me in the world. You are weak, but I am not. My strength is in You.

Lord, what is the purpose for this breathing issue? I'm confused.

Ann, the purpose is for preparation. I am fashioning you for your next assignment. Focus more on Me and less on your problem. You can breathe a sigh of relief when you breathe in Me.

Lord, I won't fret.
F Faithfully
R recalling that You are at work
E each
T time that I forget.

CHAPTER 33

Can't I Just Have Heat and Ice?

Fear not, for I am with you [Ann]; do not be dismayed,
for I am your God; I will strengthen you, I will help you,
I will uphold you with My righteous right hand.
—Isaiah 41:10 (NKJV)

Home from Mayo on Friday, and first physical therapy appointment Monday. I set my alarm, just to be sure. I had to be on time. Focus was important in physical therapy; from experience, I knew that full well. Plus, it most certainly isn't for the faint of heart. Though years had passed, I couldn't help but remember.

Ann, you have done this before and survived. Buck up. Two knee replacements. Both on the same knee. You know the drill. Bottom line? Physical therapy is not fun. Fun, no. Healing, yes. I'll press on like a good soldier.

To quote Dr. Seuss, "I do not like it, Sam I am." But I was soon to see that this wasn't like my knee replacement.

Back to the basics. Mayo's treatment plan was physical therapy three times a week for twelve weeks. Can I take it? I wasn't sure, but I wanted to survive. And thrive. The goal? To retrain my brain to realize and remember that I was capable of breathing deeply. I was ready for whatever.

But wait. I have had shallow breathing for over two years. This complicates things. My mind has decided that shallow breathing is the new normal. The assignment: to tell my brain that this is just not so. That seemed impossible. But Mayo said it was possible, with time. But how much time?

I dressed in a suitable outfit and put my running shoes on. My makeup was set. Hair in place, and ready to get this done.

The first visit caught me blindsided. My main physical therapist, Brian, asked to hear my story and then said with confidence, as he bounced out of the chair, "Let's get to work."

Work? I looked all spiffy. But *work?* What could be so difficult? It's just going to be breathing exercises, right?

My mistake. The next shoe dropped, and it wasn't my running shoe. Every exercise was designed to increase in difficulty as the days and weeks went by. Dare I say three months? This was my first day, and overwhelming didn't even describe it.

Each session began with a special breathing routine, trying to get more air into my lungs and show me that I could breathe, deeply, that is.

Breathe in through your nose as deeply as possible. Hold. Breathe out through your mouth, slower than you breathed in. Pause. Repeat five times.

Next was the stationary bike with arm movements. More minutes than I could count there. Needing a breather, I dawdled over to my next chore, I mean exercise.

The steps seemed simple. There were only a few, maybe ten, to reach the platform at the top landing. I was instructed to walk up and walk down as rapidly as possible. Thirty times, which was a total of six hundred steps. Climbing steps to nowhere seemed futile. Maybe I was climbing Mt. Everest. "I didn't want to go to Mt. Everest," I muttered to no one in particular.

On to the wall squats. Sixty of them, no less.

I sauntered over to do fifty on the bozu, which was really a hundred because of the back and forth, aforementioned. Is this a form of bait and switch? If so, I'm ready to switch.

Then I proceeded to an exam stool, complete with wheels. My directions were to scoot back and forth ten times. That will be easy-peasy. Until I realized that, drumroll please, I would do this on carpet. And ten times was really twenty. Back and forth while pushing with my heels. And it wasn't a short distance, believe me.

Being close to the part of the room where I would pass people who weren't working up a sweat, I started to ask for a shower break. Thinking that would be the worst exercise that I would encounter, I relaxed a bit. Perhaps I was on the downhill slide to victory.

A wonderful instructor came toward me next, holding what appeared to be a bag of tricks. A stopwatch emerged from the bag, and I wondered why. They would document how many times I could stand up and sit down from a chair in thirty seconds. This was unexpected but important for my patient file, I surmised.

The first day, I did it sixteen times, priding myself in doing well. By the time my twelve weeks were over, I could do it fifty-two times per set. Three sets. They allowed me to rest a minute between each set. Out of the goodness of their heart, I supposed. My TMJ is flaring up, but no one cares.

They were drill sergeants but had my best interests at heart, I guessed. Sometimes I wasn't so sure. Wasn't the hour about over?

I walked on a treadmill for ten minutes, getting faster each day. Then I finished off with another stationary bike that was set for mountain climbing.

I am not a mountain climber, I said. They smiled but either didn't hear me or chose not to listen to a wimpy woman with now drippy hair. Are you people heartless? I knew better. They really cared about me, doing their part to help me breathe correctly.

My hair and makeup looked polished and professional when I walked through the doors. I cheerfully and obediently signed in. One hour later, I was a wet noodle. *A Southern belle never looks like a wet noodle,* I thought.

The level of difficulty increased with each visit. What were they thinking? About my improvement and me, I knew. Progressing from hill climbing, I actually did end up on top of Mt. Everest. Some say. Wish I had pictures to prove it all. But I certainly couldn't hold a phone camera and trudge up the mountain at the same time.

They told me to bring an oximeter to each visit, so Al ordered me one. Placing it on my finger after each exercise, its job was to show my eyes, which then reminded the brain, that my oxygen level was excellent and my heart was beating well. I kept talking to myself all sixty minutes I was there. Remember, Ann. Retrain that brain. You can do this. The oximeter and God tell you so.

The entire focus for physical therapy was to prove to my brain that my body was capable of filling my lungs with air. The therapists weren't playing games with their part of the treatment plan. Had Mayo called and told them to work me over? Hmmm.

During these years of shallow breathing, my brain had told my body something that was incorrect: that shallow breathing would be my normal. Forever.

But no more. I was out to change the old normal to a new normal. Time would tell if this was possible.

Each day when I left the workout, I saw women whose hair and makeup still looked super, hair well-coiffed. I wasn't one of them. Many patients were on exam tables with ice on their shoulders or heat on their knees, just lollygagging around, chatting with the patient on the neighboring table. The world is not fair.

What did I get? Hair that needed help. Another shower required. No heat. And no ice. What was up with this? I asked for heat or ice. Begged on bended knee for heat or ice, in fact. Perhaps my insurance didn't cover heat or ice. I politely asked the lady at the front desk to check on that with my insurance company, but she merely smiled and walked away. Or was that a smirk?

My cries fell upon deaf ears, or so it seemed.

This all reminded me of Solomon's words in Ecclesiastes 3, with my own translation twist:

To every person there is a physical therapy season, and a time to wonder about every purpose under heaven.

A time to be born, and a time to die while there; a time to pluck myself off the exercise machines and head out the door without missing a beat.

A time to try and mutilate the therapist, and a time to rejoice that I was getting stronger; a time to break down and desire to run away, and a time to remind myself that I was building up my body while retraining my brain.

A time to lose my fear of the machines; a time to keep my cool, and a time to let the therapists know how tired I was of the difficult work.

A time to rend, tearing my body and heart apart at each grueling session and then sewing it back together, even better, with a retrained brain and a sturdy body.

A time to keep silent when I yearned to scream, "I'm tired of coming here," and a time to speak and let the therapists know how grateful I was for their assistance and encouragement.

A time to appreciate my instructors and a time to hate their cheeriness when I wasn't so cheery.

A time of wanting to challenge the other patients to war against the therapists, because they were healthy, and a time of peace, remembering that we were all there for the same goal of healing.

I was tired of the tough workouts; exhaustion followed me each time I left their torture chamber. Melted wax. That's how I felt. Although refusing to check myself out in the mirror, I knew I looked pitiful.

On the flip side, I was confident that the end goal would be healing. I wasn't smiling about it yet, though.

Twelve weeks is a long time: three months. Three times a week, an hour each session. Plus the shower, including hair washing, blow-drying, and curling iron afterward. Half a day was what it took for each visit.

Couldn't they give me a break? Instead, I thought I was having a breakdown. But I didn't have time to have a breakdown. I felt as if the wheels were falling off my truck, and I was sinking fast.

Some days, I had a positive attitude. Other days, escaping the torture became paramount. I kept glancing at the clock. The repetitions weren't easy, and I was tired before I got there. Breathing, in and of itself, was tiresome.

I had a lot of time to watch other patients. Their heat and ice looked so inviting. I was envious, to say the least.

"I'd like to have ice," I suggested pleasantly.

Each therapist's answer was a resounding, "No."

"What about heat then?" I was pulling out all the stops.

Rolling their eyes, they shuffled away to the next patient. Why weren't they listening to me? Maybe they were used to my tirades and outbursts. Possibly.

The awful abyss was much of my physical therapy experience. I was working like a dog on this part of the treatment plan but was getting nowhere fast. Nothingness is a frustrating feeling.

Some days, it felt as if PT didn't stand for physical therapy but more like perilous terror. That was a better description. Yep. I'm going with that.

I needed God's undergirding to get me through the perilous terror of each appointment.

What blessings did He provide at their office?

- Christian music playing
- Bible verses of encouragement posted
- therapists who led God-directed lives
- opportunities for me to encourage other patients

I reconciled myself to the fact that, although physical therapy was tough, God was making Ann tougher.

Like it or not, I would eat every bite of the treatment plan with a spoon, even if it tasted like castor oil.

One thing I still don't know was, why can't I have heat or ice? No one listened as I dragged my bone-tired body out the door.

Still wondering why, but heading home for a long, hot shower.

God Chair Journal Entry

Sovereign Lord,
How can you love me so much, frail creature that I am?

Ann,
I see your heart, for I created it.
I see your potential, for I instigated it.
I see your weaknesses, for I formed them.
I see your strengths, for I gave them to you.

Lord, Your love keeps lifting me higher and higher as I travel this life journey. Walking beside you, it sends me deeper and deeper in my closeness with You. And one day, heaven.

"Higher and Higher" by Jackie Wilson (my version):
Your love, God, is lifting me higher
than I've ever been lifted before.
So keep it up, God, You're my desire
And You'll be at my side forevermore.

I made you a frail creature so that you would easily see your need of Me. You are not perfect, for I do not make perfect people. Why do I not create earthly perfection? Then you would see no need for Me.

True, indeed, my Lord.

CHAPTER 34

It's Not for Wimps

Why are you cast down, O my inner self? And why should
you moan over me and be disquieted within me? Hope in
God and wait expectantly for Him, for I [Ann] shall yet praise
Him, Who is the help of my countenance and my God.
—Psalm 42:11 (AMPC)

Al would tell people that I was glad to have mandated massages on my Mayo treatment plan. "Ha ha," was the response from them all.

To that jolly joke, may I say, "Hear ye. Hear ye. The type of massage in the treatment plan is not for wimps."

Turns out that there are at least ten types of massage therapy. I would have preferred the Swedish massage to be prescribed by Mayo. I knew about that one: gentle and relaxing (or so I've heard).

Deep tissue massage is a different story. Not gentle and rarely relaxing. It's all about applying firm pressure to trigger points, using slow movements to delve into the deep layers of the muscles.

Mayo wanted it to hurt well, to do some good, so that I would get well. I saw a plethora of people during this journey. Now I was searching for a Christian masseuse, and I needed to find her fast.

I located a woman in our county who was a massage therapist and a strong believer. What I didn't know was that God had ordained us to have a godly connection. That's what I preferred, and God knew my desire.

Getting to know each other better and better at each session, we soon became friends. I love how God does that. We began to trust each other with our deeper thoughts about life.

It was great to go to Debbie's basement. And great to leave her home. Because it hurt. She used sustained strokes to change my tense tissue to a serene state of calm.

Sometimes it was quite intense. Why? To encourage unhealthy patterns to become healthy. Like physical therapy and everything else on the Mayo plan.

Before beginning each appointment, she'd ask, "What is going on with your body? Where is the tension today?"

I watched as she covered her ears as I replied with gusto, "Everywhere!" I saw her note my zeal in her file.

Debbie was my fix-it friend. Tight tissues were her enemy, and her goal was to attend to my tissue issues.

My issue was my tissue. In principle, it sounded simple, yet it was complicated. I conceded and acquiesced to her wonderful hands of horror.

Each visit revealed different needs, and she addressed each one. When I was walking out, I received my marching orders:

- Remember to drink lots of water.
- Try to take an Epsom salt bath tonight.
- Use that neck wrap after one minute in the microwave.

I never said ouch (well, almost never). A few times, I nearly cried, though. It's true that we don't change anything about us until the pain is great enough. Just the same, this was a long process, like anything worthwhile.

My neuromuscular system was learning to be different, whole, and healthy. I wanted to be whole once more, but the road to get there was excruciating and challenging.

This new God-friend, with hands of gold, taught me as I listened. "I'm doing delicate work on your trigger points, Ann." *Well, I'm about to pull the trigger*, I mumbled under my shallow breath, convinced that this wasn't for wimps.

I yearned to scream, "Stop," but decided to put on a brave face instead. I did that a lot along the way toward healing.

"Deep tissue massage is not about pushing harder, Ann. It's about each muscle and the attachment. That's why I'm using slow, sustained strokes."

Slow, Debbie had said. Didn't she know that I wanted to heal fast? Some days, I forgot to be grateful for her diligence.

With each of your strokes, I am about to have a stroke, I wearily thought, as I moaned to myself. And groaned occasionally aloud. But it was making a positive difference in my breathing, so I kept going back.

She noticed from appointment to appointment how my breathing was improving and said so, without my asking. Really? I smiled in response. What intricate bodies our Creator has fashioned, but they can get out of whack (my medical term, not hers).

God was using her hands to assist my body in the healing process. If anyone tells you that they enjoy every moment of a deep tissue massage, one of three things is true:

- They are trying to be tough,
- They are lying through their teeth, or
- They have never experienced a deep tissue massage.

Debbie's massage techniques were wonderfully awful some days. But the goal of watching knots vanish was well worth the pain. I would have preferred "poof" and it's gone, but no one gave me that option. Ever.

"Ann, the pain is purposeful." In a few sessions, I visualized vicious waves, angry oceans, and roaring waterfalls as my sweet friend tested the mean waters of my tight neck and shoulders. I was carrying the world on my shoulders, yet even a firstborn could learn to lighten the load.

"Ann, there are angry issues today," Debbie would tell me. As she worked, I concurred with her assessment. The goal is for the gnarly knots to exit, stage right, as Snagglepuss, on the Yogi Bear cartoon of my youth, would say.

Lord, I'm giving all the physical, emotional, mental, and spiritual pain to You. On the way home from an appointment, God and I were chatting. *Do you see the white flag, Lord? It's raised. I surrender.* He clapped for me, understanding how difficult my health path was becoming. I could give up my plan and give in to His better plan.

Healing was hard work. It always is, but I had no choice if I wanted to heal. And I did. When I got home from a session, sometimes Al would say, encouragingly, "How was your massage today?" More than a few times, I directed a glare toward him. I wanted to hold up my white flag and respond through my ever-so-tense TMJ jaw, "Please don't ask if you don't want to know." But I kept quiet and attempted a gracious grin.

Silently, I was thinking, *This is not fun.*

But when I opened my mouth to say those thoughts aloud, Al had walked out of the room. How dare he leave before the beginning of my well-planned dissertation?

I screamed inside with all I could muster, *"Knot" fun.*

With the water filling the tub, I verbalized my dismay in a whiny whisper as I poured the Epsom salts into the hot water. I felt the bathroom steam up, just like my steamed-up thoughts. Watching the vapor make its way to the ceiling, I yearned to fly up with it.

Then I surrendered to the reality that this wasn't a zip-a-dee-doo-dah joyride. The water was hot, and the tub was full. I reconciled myself to the truth that I didn't always get what I wanted at the massage appointments. Yet I got what I needed, reminding myself that God works the same way.

Ahh. Time to soothe those gnarly knots.

Knowing that He was providing what I needed, I gingerly slipped into the Epsom salts with delight.

I surrender, Lord. I really do.

God Chair Journal Entry

Sovereign Lord,
Please forgive me. I had a mild pity party, as You well know. I was focusing on the difficulty of my tense breathing challenge instead of how Your arms are around me through this hard, long process of restoration.

Ann, I love you always, unconditionally. If you had the ability to be perfect, I still couldn't love you more. Just keep running to my arms, for I'll always be waiting for you. So keep coming to your God chair, and it will always "be well with your soul."

Lord,
I take my refuge in You. Keep talking, and I'll keep listening.

Ann, I love how you rest in My competent hands, realizing that you are safe. Since I am your Potter, I will mold you into My image.

Practice Patience

God's name is "I AM," not "I was" or "I might be" or "I may
get to it." He's in control. Always has been. Always will be.
—Jordan Riley

Charles Dickens wrote, "It was the best of times, it was the worst of times."
That was how I felt about working Mayo's treatment plan.

Toes tapping while waiting in line to check in for physical therapy.
Knees knocking while at a stoplight, almost late to another acupuncture
session. Walking to yoga class in the rain. This Mayo Treatment Plan train
was dizzying me. Stop this train. Let me off at the next station, please.

Bah, humbug. I'm ready to scream. Silently, of course. "Ann, you don't
scream." Control yourself. Stay stoic.

I give up, Lord. He lovingly replied, "Finally. Ann, that is progression.
You are not standing still, even though it may feel that way. Don't you
recall the view I gave you when you got on your knees, as a young married
lady, and repented for closing Me out?"

It was easy to remember that time because He had indelibly engraved
it into my memory. I flashed back, recalling how eager I was, as a
twentysomething girl, wanting a baby so badly that it hurt.

Young, married, and teaching third grade. Could it really be forty-five
years ago? I came home that day, having had enough of myself. Getting
on my knees, I looked up at a beautiful blue sky dotted with fluffy white
clouds and prayed, "I am tired of being angry at You, building a wall to

separate us. I choose to trust that Your way is better than mine. All I ask is that You not let my pain be in vain."

I was crying out to Him about my infertility and yearning for a child to hold. And love. And nurture. This wasn't hard for God. Why is He waiting while I'm hurting?

I had to practice patience then, I vividly remembered. *Can I practice patience now, with this breathing bedlam?*

Was I up for another wait? I am older and less patient.

"Ann, you've walked through tough things in the past in My strength. Don't you realize that I am with you now, as well?"

How quickly we forget when life isn't going our way. *Yes, Lord, You are here.* I recalled that blue sky with white fluffy clouds the first time I sat in my God chair.

In the midst of infertility pain, You came through by giving us two precious children. You will come through now for me, as I sit before You. Seriously sit before the God of my patience. In my God chair. You were worth the wait then, Lord, so You are worth the wait now.

My cluttered thoughts went on another vein. *Can a fish be bored? My guess is no, but I can. Be bored, I mean. Waiting on the Lord. Why is practicing patience so important?*

Then I remembered. There is a cross in my car. Our granddaughter made it for me. It's a visual reminder of the truth. Christ died for the painful situation in which I find myself. Every situation. Then I was in my twenties. Now in my sixties.

Grabbing my phone and scrolling through some old texts, I found it. There was the comfort I needed for that day. Right in my phone. I read it aloud, very slowly, sensing the importance of not rushing through the healing words. Encouragement sent from a friend:

"You, Ann, may heal slowly because you have done so much already all of your life, and you need to rest a little longer before He gives you something else to do. And while you are resting, you are showing others how to wait on God's timing, which is a difficult thing for humans. He is still using you. So just rest up to do His next assignment."

Ouch. Sometimes the truth hurts in order to help. Millie's text reminded me to relax when I wanted to rebel instead.

As children, Mama drilled into our brains that it didn't take any intelligence to be on time. I can't argue with you, Mama. If you were still on earth, you would probably add, "Ann, God can take as long as He wants. After all, He knows the right time for everything. So practice patience."

That's true. He knew the right time for Al and me to become parents. Surely, I can trust His timing for this breathing madness. And learn the important lesson of patience at the same time, even if it feels, on some days, like the crowning blow. The icing on the proverbial cake.

Was this illness an unmitigated disaster or a divine gift? I wrestled patiently for an answer, but He wasn't revealing anything yet. Impatience once again from me, His impatient child. Sometimes, I run. Sometimes, I crawl. And sometimes, I run into a brick wall. A strong wall of fighting what I know I should do. Or be.

You, Lord, have told me repeatedly that You created human beings, not human doings.

Ahh. So being patient must mean that I have to be. Be in my God chair. To listen. And just be. Alone with my thoughts and with You. It's so simple yet extraordinarily complicated.

Lord, You could have set out a shorter route for the Israelites. They had a long journey too yet had many useful things to learn. Like me. About patience.

I was driving one day, contemplating all of this being stuff, when there it was. While at a traffic light, I saw a bumper sticker on the car in front of me that read "RESIST."

"You are resisting, Ann."

Am I? Really?

"You are. Really."

And You will drag me into resting even if I'm kicking and screaming, right?

"Yes, ma'am, I'll indeed do so because I love you that much."

I reluctantly, yet patiently, attempted a smile.

Well, I've always grown when You have forced me to be. And to be patient. May I be honest? I still want to scream, Lord.

"Go ahead, Ann. Scream away. Patiently, if you can."

This was the best of times and the worst of times.

But God could teach.

Even me.

God Chair Journal Entry

Sovereign Lord,

You give me many opportunities to practice patience, especially during this seemingly never-ending breathing challenge. You must be preparing me for something special.

Ann, I always prepare you. In fact, you might say that "Preparation Practice" is My middle name.

So, Lord, I guess you are in charge of just how long the patience wait will be for me.

Ann, many times, you are not ready to receive what I have ordained for you. That's when I press the pause button, causing you to pause for patience as part of your preparation practice.

Then this preparation practice course prepares me to be ready to receive Your next assignment, Sir?

You are as right as rain, Ann. Visualize this healing process as a beautiful opportunity to practice patience. And staying in My presence in your God chair is invaluable in the process.

Always remember, My daughter, that the best is yet to come.

Lord, one day, perhaps I won't be surprised by Your surprises.

CHAPTER 36

This Mess Is a Place

As I struggle with all my might to be sure to get things right.
—Martha B. Morgan, *My Life*

This mess is a place—or is it that this place is a mess? Don't know. Don't care. I had no energy, so lots of things at home fell by the wayside. My get-up-and-go had got up and went, as the old folks say. "The only way to do it is to do it." I had heard that motivational comment somewhere before in another context. But I didn't want to do it, whatever it happened to be at any given moment. What an inadequate feeling when once upon a time, I was so organized and could keep it all together. Previously, but not now. What a mess I found myself in.

And don't tell me that you are one of those people who fold fitted sheets when they emerge from the dryer, placing them ever so neatly in your linen closet. One day, when I was really bored, I watched a YouTube video on folding fitted sheets properly. I laughed all the way to the end of the video and then went on my merry way.

While I knew that God had placed me in this breathing mess in order for me to grow in Him, learn from Him, and lean upon Him, I still had to look at the house. I was a fairly tidy person until my once-sufficient breath left the building with Elvis.

The mess was getting deeper, along with my somber spirit. My sweet husband took up the slack, which made me feel loved. Al cared so much, and he was quite concerned. On the other hand, I felt sad. Why wasn't I helping him? I wanted to join in the clean-up brigade but just couldn't. It was a woman thing. I yearned to feel useful at home, but I wasn't. Ever. Or so I felt.

Juggling appointments, while continuing to put all the little energy I possessed into my day job, made even my semiorganized brain spin. Why can't I give myself a break without feeling guilty? Balance. Balance. I kept saying that word to myself, hoping that it would sink in.

The mess was a place in my mind; I struggled to see light at the end of my terrible tunnel of torture, but it was nowhere to be seen. *Did it even exist? Is it realistic to think it will ever happen?* Those were some of my rambling thoughts, at every turn.

Yep. An overloaded mind. That was my self-diagnosis, and it sounded very professional. What kept my head above water was Al's consistent help to keep the house in order as well as his strong arms, which held up my arms that were weak and weary. There were many Moses/Aaron moments in our home.

Thankfully, when I sat in my God chair each day, all the mess in my mind and the mess in our house melted away. In His presence is fullness of joy, the Bible reminds us. *How true*, I thought, as I settled down in the blue wing-backed chair once more. I was sitting at the feet of Jesus, in the arms of my heavenly Father. No agenda. No pressure to perform. What a delight.

Unlike my counselors, God never gave me homework. He was just glad to see me show up, and we often talked without words. He would smile at me, and I would glory in His creation, especially when the weather was pleasant, and I left the blue chair to head for our deck.

"Ann, don't be frustrated when you are unable to help Al around the house. Didn't he say, just last week, when you mentioned to him that you appreciated how helpful he was, 'Ann, don't thank me. I should have been doing this throughout our marriage.' You see, your breathing lessons haven't been just for you. I am growing your husband along this journey as well."

What? Al too? Reminding me, once again, what an all-inclusive God I serve. It sounds as if "we trust You" starts with "I trust You." With me. With Al. With everyone.

Reluctantly, but realistically, I saw His Truth, almost watching the scales being removed from my eyes. "Don't try to do everything, Ann,"

God revealed to my heart. "Why would you think I meant for you to do it all? I created families to bear one another's burdens and so fulfill the law of Christ. You remember that verse. Rest in My sovereignty over you, and rest in Al's love for you. He wants to help, so let him. Stop being so strong. Even better, maybe you will even cry a bit."

Thinking of a newspaper article I had read years ago titled "It's Clean Enough," I smiled at God for bringing it to my remembrance. Martha had mailed those words of encouragement to me. We both felt better, knowing that our houses and our minds were just fine, thank you very much, even with more than a few dust bunnies under the sofa and an occasional ring around the toilet. I got it. And so did she. We weren't created for perfection on earth. "I'm a mess without Him and I'm in a mess without Him."

God must have been confident that I had learned another lesson because He returned my grin with a wink and a thumbs-up.

God Chair Journal Entry

Sovereign Lord,
What was Your purpose in creating Palmetto bugs (cockroaches)?

The exterminator came to put a syringe of thick poison around the baseboard of the deck. He said the bugs would come out of the trees at nightfall, eat a tiny amount of the poison, and crawl back into the trees to die.

I didn't know they lived in the beautiful trees around the deck, Lord. When I'm outside during the day, they hide from my view. How was I to know what they did after dark?

The trees hide the bugs, Ann, as the deceiver of your soul hides his evil angels wanting to infiltrate your life deck. Because I am the Exterminator, I squeeze the poison of protection around your life deck so that the evil angels won't destroy you on your spiritual growth walk with Me.

Lord, thank You for being my Protector even when I don't know that I need protecting.

Ann, you usually don't know when I'm protecting you. Let the reality of that gift soak in.

CHAPTER 37

Soul-Itude: Permission to Rest

The Lord is my [Ann's] Shepherd, I lack nothing. He
makes me to lie down in green pastures, He leads me
beside quiet waters. He refreshes my soul.
—Psalm 23:1–3a (NIV)

How could I forget that day? I was simply driving to my massage therapist, minding my own business. About a month into the Mayo Treatment Plan, it happened.

I was at a traffic light, not thinking any particular God-thoughts. Or any thoughts really. I could make the drive in my sleep, only I wasn't dozing. You may recall that I don't sleep sitting up.

Right in the car, all alone, God revealed words to my heart when He knew I was ready to listen.

There was no radio on. Nothing to hear but the sounds of my car and His still, small, powerful voice. He spoke just to me.

"Ann, I have ordained this time as a gift of soul-itude for you. Enjoy it and learn of Me."

I frantically grabbed a pen and a scrap of paper from the bottom of my purse. "You can't forget this," I mumbled nervously.

I hastily jotted down His exact words before the light changed to green; a car behind me honked their horn.

I had lived for many years on the fast track of life, sailing past others who were slower drivers. Me, the one who was around people constantly for twenty-five years. It was essential to my job description.

From patients, to staff, to donors, to board members, to speaking in churches, to encouraging middle and high school students in a health class to choose sexual integrity. It fit the gifting God had given to me. I had been the Energizer Bunny, but not breathing had slowed me down. What a difference between then and now.

Does true living mean doing less and being more?

Then I noted that the God of my fast life was giving me permission to rest. After all, He had just told me to "enjoy it," hadn't He? And it was a command, not a suggestion.

When He told me to "learn of Him" during this time of isolation, He knew that I liked to learn new things.

I was isolated from people by physical therapy appointments, counseling sessions, yoga classes, acupuncture, and deep tissue massage. All were a part of Mayo's assignments for my healing but lovingly delivered by God.

Martha joked that it was my new full-time job. It was a true statement, to be sure. She told me that before my illness, it wasn't an easy feat to walk through the grocery store with me, as it seemed like a track meet, the way I was sprinting along. And I was out to win the race.

God was taking me away to a place of quiet by immersing me in the pleasure of being with Him. His current plan was to renew my soul as I pressed into Him. Surprisingly, I enjoyed my soul-itude because my soul was at rest. I had permission to stop.

Was He stopping me from doing good things for His best things? *Hmmm.* Sounds like *Him.*

I pondered for a moment. Can I really rest if I don't first stop something? That made sense. Relax and renew seemed to be His calling on me right now.

Soul-itude. Soul-rest. I'm a sojourning soldier in serious need of solace. No argument there.

Lord, You must know the depth of my need. But did I know how thirsty I was for rest with Him? I felt deliriously dazzled, yet questioning my thoughts.

I wondered if my thirst could be quenched, until I accepted His restoration through rest.

You know, Lord, that relaxing doesn't come easy for this fireball, hard driver, power horse, stick of dynamite. Called all of those phrases at different points in my life, I knew they were terms of endearment. Some personalities make resting more difficult, I contemplated, struggling to take a deep breath. God loved me too much to leave me as a bouncing bunny. He was calling me to be a restful rabbit. And I didn't even mind that He hid my batteries.

Before I knew it, I was parking in front of my massage therapist's home. A twinkle in my eyes. A song in my heart. A lift in my step. And permission to rest.

That's what You have prepared for me. A generous gift just for my soul. Soul-itude.

I stuffed the notes I had taken at the stoplight into a safe spot in my purse. I got out of the car, looked up to heaven, and smiled. Soul-itude. I'll enjoy it. It will be good for my soul. I'll learn of You.

Soaking in soul-itude may actually be more beneficial that soaking in Epsom salts.

How could I think that I had a breathing calamity? It's a heavenly calm-ity. What soul-itude. (But bring on the Epsom salts, just for good measure.)

God Chair Journal Entry

Sovereign Lord,

You have given me Your solitude so that I can have soul-itude. You are doing deep things in my soul during this time of solitary soul-searching that You have ordained for me.

Ann, enjoy this time and learn of Me. Cherish this refreshing joy to be quiet, to rest, to be alone (but not lonely). The condition of your soul is always paramount to Me.

"(You're My) Soul and Inspiration" by the Righteous Brothers (my version):
You're my soul and my highest inspiration.
You're all I've got to get me by.
You're my soul and my highest inspiration.
Without you, God,
What good am I?
What good am I?

Thank You for being my "soul-keeper." You give me joy.

J Joyfully
O overwhelmed by
Y Your grace.

Ann, you can always catch your breath and grab your joy when you stop long enough to breathe Me in.

CHAPTER 38

My Wonderful Wilderness

Behold, [Ann,] I am doing a new thing; now it springs forth, do you not
perceive it? I will make a way in the wilderness and rivers in the desert.
—Isaiah 43:19 (RSV)

On first glance, the desert doesn't appear to be a wonderland of fun. Hot,
sandy, windy, dry. Suffice it to say, I would need a ton of moisturizer every
day, as would you. Some days, I felt like a tumbleweed, blowing across the
desert of not breathing well.

That changed when God spoke to me in the car. "Ann, I have ordained
this as a time of soul-itude. Enjoy it and learn of me." That's why I started
telling friends that I was in a wonderful wilderness. The phrase fit.

The looks I got, you wouldn't believe. Taken aback, people didn't know
how to respond. They knew I was in a tough spot. A petrified piece of
wood, maybe. But a wonderful wilderness? Their faces revealed confusion,
and the teacher in me was quick to explain.

"God is teaching me wonderful things in my wonderful wilderness," I
followed up immediately, hoping they would understand. After all, I did.
But then I was living the journey, clinging to Him, but with no break in
the action. It had become my life.

I would continue, "He yearns to do a wonderful work in my wonderful
wilderness as I rest in the knowledge that He is always up to something
good."

Although that added description helped, many people still looked
unsettled, but I didn't know what else to say.

"Ann, these people have not walked a mile in your moccasins. Just tell them what I am doing in your life, and let Me work in their wilderness. After wandering awhile, they will see that a wonderful wilderness is a deeper relationship with Me."

Thank You, Lord, for lovingly placing me—*kerplop*—in my very own wonderful wilderness. Your plans for me are always good. I rest and relax in that knowledge, most of the time. When I remember.

"Ann, you are human, so give yourself a break. I give you breaks all the time. Do the same for yourself."

Each lap of this track meet is teaching me so much, Lord.

"Ann, you are in My process of preparation place. It's a wilderness of wonder, because I have future assignments for you that demand this time of learning."

Some days, Lord, the highs are awfully wonderful. The lows, really awful. Not boring, though, I must say.

"Ann, I am never a boring God. You can take that to the bank. And to the wilderness."

I thank You for this desert gift of isolation, engaging me, or was it forcing me, to be quiet, hearing You as never before.

"Stopping people in their tracks is one of My most-used tactics, Ann. I got your attention, didn't I? Now you are on a fast track, although it may appear slow to you, learning how to rest in Me."

Who knew I was that teachable?

"I did, Ann. Remember that I have known you before the foundation of the world. And rest assured, you won't remain in this dry valley of shallow breath forever. I am the One Who brings refreshing rain to your soul."

Lord, my friend told me that the death-to-self walk is really the victory walk, and I agree. In this wonderful wilderness, I feel at peace with You. Whether You choose to heal me in this world or the next, all is well.

At first, the blowing sand in my wilderness stung my face, as well as my focus; some days, it didn't feel wonderful. All I wanted to do was pass the wilderness exam so I could move on with my life. Yet I chose to believe what He was doing in me was beyond wonderful.

I received a Wonderful Wilderness (WW) degree from God's School of Hard Knocks. Here are some of the classes I took in my WW University:

- WW 101. Don't knee jerk. Do let God settle you.
- WW 201. Don't talk so much. Do listen to Him.
- WW 301. Don't lean on the good in you. Do lean on the Good Shepherd.
- WW 401. Don't "be" a god. Do "be with" God.
- WW 501. Don't forge ahead. Do give up and give in.
- WW 601. Don't go in your strength. Do rest in His strength.
- WW 701. Don't ask a lot. Do thank a lot.

What a refreshing time. This wonderful wilderness is a gift and a plan from the Best Planner of them all.

For me. At this time.

To prepare me for more.

And I don't have to know what.

I just have to say yes. And I say yes to You.

Sitting in the God chair, relishing the classes in my Wonderful Wilderness, and holding a cornucopia of blessings, I sighed.

I may even have taken a deep breath.

God Chair Journal Entry

Sovereign Lord,
There is a pale, silvery sky right now. Not gray but not blue and not white, either. It feels as if I could just float up to heaven because there seems to be no top, no ceiling to the sky today.

You know my heart, Lord. I would be happy to float on up to be with You and my family and friends who have gone before me.

You know the reasons I say that. My energy level is low, and I have aches and pains that seem as if they won't go away.

I suppose that You must not be ready to take me home today. You aren't finished with me yet.

You have shown me that You do wonderful work in my wonderful wilderness, and I rest in that promise.

But it's still not easy. Easy will be heaven. No aches, no pains, no breathing issues, no low energy, no waiting, just reveling in Your goodness and rejoicing before the throne.

I'm looking forward to it.

I've done all of the talking today. Thanks for listening, Lord.

Little Annie Rooney, I never tire of hearing your voice. And it's a blessing that you never tire of My voice, either.

Thank You Lord, that I don't have to be anxious about the gift of being broken.

CHAPTER 39

In the Trenches with Him

We destroy arguments and every lofty opinion raised against the
knowledge of God, and take every thought captive to obey Christ.
—2 Corinthians 10:5 (ESV)

The Mayo doctors explained that I had developed a rut in my brain, telling
my body that I wasn't capable of breathing correctly. A rut is a pattern of
behavior that has become unproductive and difficult to change. I read one
time that the only difference between a rut and a grave is the depth.

"To assist with that process, Ann, seek out a professional who
specializes in cognitive behavioral therapy." My assignment was to locate
this counselor.

I didn't connect with the word *rut*, so "trench" became my word to
express it.

Why had that word resonated with me, as opposed to rut? I learned
that a trench is a long, narrow ditch used by soldiers as a place of shelter
from enemy fire. Ah hah.

Leaning back in my chair to let that information soak in, I pondered
the knowledge that I had an enemy who was the deceiver of my soul. It was
evident that I needed a place of shelter from his evil attacks. I understood.
A rut is purposeless, like a dead end getting me nowhere but to defeat. A
trench is purposeful, leading to growth and victory and, for me, healing.

*God, I want to fill the trenches in my brain with all of You, but what does
that visually look like, Sir?*

I immediately visualized a picture of our front yard. A six-inch-deep by four-inch-wide trench ran across the yard, from side to side. God was standing on one side of the trench, while I was on the other side. Since we were only a couple of feet apart, I could see His face clearly, feeling enveloped in His glory.

He was dressed in a long, white robe; dazzling light was all around His clothing and His head. It was spectacular, amazing. As He smiled deeply into my eyes, I quickly noticed that His large, strong hands held an open Bible. I then saw that my hands held a stack of white, 3-by-5 notecards and a blue pen.

What was going on? I wasn't certain, but I felt "calm, cool and collected," as Mama used to say. I watched myself writing a promise from God's Word on each of the cards. As I completed each one, slowly holding it over the trench, I glanced into His eyes before I let it go. He nodded approvingly.

Thinking it would fall straight down, I jumped a little when the card floated like a feather, gently and effortlessly making its travel into the trench. It was mesmerizing to view each one fall into its own special place. The trench was filling up with His words for Ann and no one else.

Wow. I really could retrain my brain. He had revealed His plan to me through this simple, yet profound example.

"Lord, you are seldom early but never late," I mused, confident that my brain would heal completely one day.

I eagerly anticipated my next counseling session to tell DeAnn about the visual message God had revealed. She enjoyed hearing what God was doing in my life, and I was thrilled to share it.

As the session came to an end, I got my homework assignment: "Ann, this week, choose a Bible verse to recite every time the negative voices rear their ugly heads, trying to defeat the healing progress."

I've had many negative thoughts in my life, as has everyone. It's part of the human experience as well as the deceiver's ploy. What I didn't know until my stint at Mayo was that horribly destructive 3-by-5 cards had filled up my brain, forming a restless rut.

"Will I ever get well?"

"I'm so exhausted."

"Can I function at work again tomorrow?"

"Will my breathing stay this way until heaven?"

My counselor's words resonated in my head: "Ann, whatever you think about the most will grow."

Every time I had allowed those defeating thoughts to win the day, the rambling rut got deeper. And I had been doing that for the better part of three years. I was digging my own hole, unknowingly. But no more. I had a mission to retrain my brain, and I knew that I would accomplish the mission in the strength of God and the promises in His Word. After all, He was in the trench beside me, wiping my perspiring brow.

As I drove home from the counseling session, the first negative thought bubbled up, eager and waiting for my permission to let it come out. Just in the nick of time, I squelched it with God's help and His Word.

Ann, remember, I lectured myself repeatedly. *Whatever you think about the most will grow, so fill the trench with Him.*

I was determined. Focused. Armed to fight the deceiver of my soul. *The rotten rut won't receive negative Miracle Gro soil from me. No sirree. I live in trench world now, with Him as my personal Commander in charge.*

My traumatic health event was August 6, 2015.

"Ann, trauma is involuntary, but the negative brain result is the same." I was taking notes as fast as I could write during each counseling appointment.

My body had been in control of my brain. Now I have the tools to retrain my brain. It will return to being in control of my body, my breathing. *Whew. My hurting hand can't write much more. But I have to remember that my brain will relearn.*

On weaker days, my mind wanted to give up and give in to the weariness of it all. This is not a walk in the park.

Strong Ann would then remember another quote:

> Sometimes the last place I want to go is
> exactly where God wants me to be.
> —Joseph E. Miller

There is never a situation bigger than God. He is larger than life, and I serve that God. My silent breathing pain had rambled in my brain for way too long, causing a negative rut that I was working hard each day to convert into a trench. God would fight with me in the trench, tooth and nail. Together, God and I were armed and ready to fight all negatives.

Lord, in the trenches with You is where I choose to remain. That is my true calling, I thought as I fluffed my pillow, settling into my warm bed that night. I recalled the vision of meeting with God in the front yard, seeing all of His glory. What a heavenly experience.

Him. Only Him. In the trenches. I was writing verses on 3-by-5 cards. Watching them float. Seeing Him smile.

Mayo was correct that a rut is a negative path. But God was teaching me that a trench is the place where I remain still and fight the good fight, with Him by my side in the trenches with me. He and I would win this war. The deceiver was mad, so I was glad.

All God. All guiding.

What a marvelous mystery.

Watching Him work.

God Chair Journal Entry

Sovereign Lord,
I enjoy my deck God chair with You.
The blowing breeze reminds me that You are giving me a second wind.
You lovingly took away my first wind in order to give me something better.

When I asked You why I wasn't back to normal, you clearly said,

"Ann, You will never go back to where You were. I have greater plans. Your new 'normal' will be better than your former 'normal.' Remember that the leaf withereth, and the flower fadeth away, but the Word of the Lord remains forever."

Lord, my life pilgrimage sends me to steep paths on a spiritual adventure with You.

Ann, when the deceiver comes your way, trying to attack you with his big guns, just stay in the trenches with Me, and you will always be able to fight the good fight.

The former Ann is fading away, but Your Words, which I will tell the world, will remain forever.

CHAPTER 40

Lavender's Blue, Dilly Dilly

For the Lord your God is living among you, [Ann]. He is a mighty
Savior. He will take delight in you with gladness. With His love, He
will calm all your fears. He will rejoice over you with joyful songs."
—Zephaniah 3:17 (NLT)

I recall hearing Burl Ives sing "Lavender's Blue, Dilly Dilly" when I was
young. It was on our black-and-white television. He is long gone now, but
I still can hear his unique, kind voice as he sang. And the beard. Along
with that winsome smile.

The Oxford English Dictionary defines *dilly* as "an excellent example of
a particular type of person or thing." It comes from an obsolete adjective
meaning "delightful," and I found her at a Mayo appointment. She
introduced me to lavender.

Before heading to Minnesota, I had no awareness of essential oils. But
someone on the medical staff told me about the benefits, and I have been
using it ever since. Remember that I had anointed my hotel room with oil
given to me by a friend.

I certainly had no clue that there was a lavender farm a short drive
from our home. It turns out that June is the month for blooming. Al
and I ventured to it on a Saturday morning excursion. It was close to my
birthday, so I purchased lavender linen spray for bedtime, natural lavender
deodorant, lavender milk bubble bath, and lavender bath salts. Al was
delighted that he didn't have to wonder what gift to give me. Mission
accomplished for him.

Did I go overboard by getting so much? My frugal self silently questioned the purchases.

Forcefully and courageously, I answered my question with, "Desperate times call for desperate measures." I was desperate for healing, by any means necessary. I retorted back to myself a "so there," as I commanded the items to find their spot in the bag.

Lavender has a variety of uses, and Deb encouraged me to use it. "Basically, Ann, it is believed to provide a calming effect to the central nervous system." That sold me immediately. This breathing issue had left little calmness to be had. I learned that the shallow breathing caused my body to stay in an anxious, exhausted state.

Though breathless, I was writing this new information on a Mayo notepad. This health issue has certainly caused me to be anxious and restless, and to wake up during the night, so I was all in for trying the lavender. Actually, I was willing to try anything. Deb leaned over her desk, grabbed the lavender mist spray sitting near the edge, and placed it in my hand.

"Spray your hotel room," was her suggestion. So we did. Religiously. For all ten days at Mayo. When I would forget, Al remembered. He was the last in bed and would spray all around the area before he joined me as we settled in for a short winter's nap.

When we got back home, Al surprised me with an infuser, placing it by the chair where I always sat.

For Christmas, my massage therapist gave me a lavender aromatherapy roll-on. I kept it in my purse to place on my wrists when I was out and about. Someone even said there was a lavender hand sanitizer. I'm still looking for it.

I had heard that you can't teach an old dog new tricks. Well, this older dog was learning to retrain her brain. I'll do this thing. My ferocious will can overcome my brain, I bravely remembered.

I am adept at being Courageous Ann.

Can I also be Calm Ann?

I pondered thoughts like that as I sprayed the Sweet Dream Linen Spray on our sheets each evening when we returned home from Mayo. Getting ready for bed, I read on the label "Made with lavender essential oil, known for its soothing and relaxing benefits." I sighed as I breathed in the comforting smell.

Tumbling into bed, I prayed that I would sleep soundly.

Perhaps Courageous Ann could be Calm Ann someday.

I yawned, thinking it strange to put courage and calm in the same thought process.

But just maybe it was possible. After all, God can do anything. His Word says that He made a donkey talk. Surely turning me into Calm Ann would be a cinch.

Before I zoned out, I chuckled, "And the lavender can't hurt."

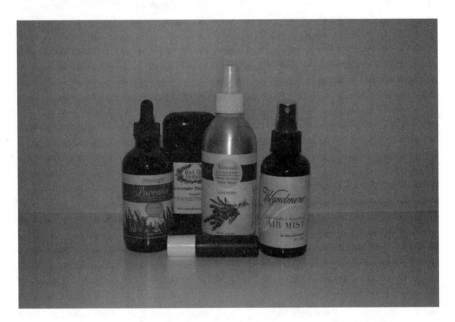

God Chair Journal Entry

Sovereign Lord,

Al made me feel loved this week by bringing me jar candles. He knows that I enjoy the lingering smell and the flickering wick. You give even better gifts, gifts that I often walk by without noticing. Like the wet leaves on the deck after this rainy week. They are doing nothing, yet they remind me of being calm. Calm in my God chair. I want to collapse into Your calm, Lord. Drench me.

Ann, the deeper you linger with Me, the calmer you get. Collapsing into My calm is not a sign of weakness. It takes courage to be calm. Remain calm, Ann.

Lord, even when life hurts my heart?

Yes, Ann. Even then.

That's hard, Lord.

Your cup overflows with calmness when you realize that I am the only One who can fill you with calm, courageous calm.

_C_ Courageously, yet with calmness,
_A_ at every turn,
_L_ leaning on my
_M_ majestic Lord.

CHAPTER 41

Real but Not True

So we fix our eyes not on what is seen, but on what is unseen,
since what is seen is temporary, but what is unseen is eternal.
—2 Corinthians 4:18 (NIV)

Tsoknyl Rinpoche coined the phrase "real but not true," and my counselor, DeAnn, first heard it from a psychologist, Dr. Tara Brach. I became a beneficiary of that knowledge.

At Mayo, I learned that my shallow breathing, which never went away, even in my sleep, was quite real in my body but not the truth. My lungs worked fine, and no one could ask for a better oxygen level. Yet I still wasn't breathing normally, and it was an exhausting way to live. Every doctor at Mayo had understood my turmoil and wanted to help.

Ann, you are an intelligent woman. How could this happen? I often said this to myself, in a confused sort of way. *What a predicament. I feel lost, between a rock and a hard place, in a most difficult situation.* Was I sparring with myself? If so, I think I'm losing the contest.

Then I remembered. At the pregnancy center, we heard sad stories of women who had past abortions. Adamantly, they would describe their hurt in these words: "God couldn't forgive me for what I've done."

To them, that was a fact in their heart and mind. A reality to them but not truth. We would gently reveal the truth, that God forgives everything when we address Him with a repentant and contrite heart. Many times, I had wondered why that great news was so difficult for women to wrap their head around, as well as their heart. *They should be elated to receive the truth*, I thought, frustrated.

Then God revealed to me another situation of people who were in a "real but not true" quandary. A man comes home from war with a severed leg, convinced, beyond any doubt, that there is pain in his leg. Yet there is no leg. The physical suffering is powerfully real to his mind but not the least bit true.

The brain is complex, like all the intricate organs that God has placed into our bodies. He is the majestic, marvelous maker of us.

Mama received her Alzheimer's diagnosis in Charleston, SC, at age seventy. She lived ten years longer. Our family watched as her brain slowly faded. Medications offered a helping hand, but the end of that disease is death. Alzheimer's is real as well as true.

"Ann, your issue is different. You can recover. Completely."

Once again, I watched God be my cheerleader.

Our mind and our body are very connected. One can tell the other what is real. But perhaps it's not the truth.

Then another example came to mind. Someone who is anorexic can look in a mirror and see an obese image staring back. Real, but not true.

"Ann, it will take time. Perhaps a great deal of time to retrain your brain." Hearing those encouraging words while at Mayo and from my local counselor, I wasn't sure if God was being my cheerleader once more or perhaps I was now cheering myself along. It didn't matter because I was encouraged.

Wow. I have the ability to build a brand-new neural pathway. I have the power, and it all begins in my mind. They can retrain the brains of people with learning disabilities and other neurological disorders. So I wasn't alone on this journey. Others had walked it as well.

I recalled a Mayo doctor who had said, "I wish you had gotten to us sooner. Two and a half years is a long time to breathe incorrectly, Ann."

Convinced that it would be a long walk up the steep mountain, I prepared myself spiritually, mentally, emotionally, and physically as I focused on the goal line.

"Ann," I lectured myself, "when you change your thoughts, all will be well, literally." I surmised that if I was going to correct my breathing pattern, I had to change my thinking pattern.

Reality check. I don't have a raspberry seed in my back tooth. That would merely require some good ole flossing and would be a quick fix. Voilà. But this issue is more complicated because I've been breathing incorrectly for a long time. My brain has told my body that shallow breathing is a new normal forever, and I had to train my brain to believe that it was wrong.

The deceiver thinks he has me in a crossfire. He loses. I win because God wins. Jostled? Yes. Defeated? No.

When I got into bed that night, I felt calm. His calm. I'm stronger. At the starting line. No longer afraid of the difficult trauma work ahead. Then I heard Daddy's voice in my ear. He lives two hours away, so it couldn't be him. It didn't matter. He said it so often that I could recite it easily. The prayer.

"Thank you, Lord, for the situation in which I find myself, knowing that Your perfect plan will be worked out."

I needed that reminder, Lord.

That's real. And the truth. Your Truth.

Lord, I also could use a pound of patience as I pound the pavement on this hard road to recovery.

And could you send it by overnight express?

God Chair Journal Entry

Sovereign Lord,
The ivy is climbing up this large tree in three distinct directions. What are You saying?

Ann, the ivy is killing the tree. The ivy and the tree cannot coexist. If the ivy lives, the tree dies. If the tree is to live, the ivy must die.

There is past ivy on you that must die, so you can truly live in the way I have ordained for you.

Although the counseling sessions are difficult, I know you want to live an abundant life. But that isn't possible with ivy choking the life out of you.

So rejoice in the sessions. They are a part of My provision to destroy the death you've been dragging around so that you can be a tall tree, strong and victorious. Then you will be fully alive and refreshed, ever attuned to hear my next assignment, aligned to join Me in My work.

"[Ann] is like a tree planted along the riverbank, bearing fruit each season. Her leaves never wither, and she prospers in all that she does" (my version of Psalm 1:3 NLT).

CHAPTER 42

Pants and Needles

Now my neck begins to ache ... and my nerves might start to break.
—Martha B. Morgan, *My Work*

I chuckled when my yoga instructor said, with a mischievous smile, "It's more than the pants."

My yoga pants were several years old, but I had never done yoga in them. Most people don't. They are merely comfy pants for home. Am I right?

That is until Mayo Clinic and the treatment plan. Yoga will help you breathe deeply and relax, they had said. Me? Relax? That would be a tall order.

The first yoga referral was to a private instructor. My friend, Lynn, a former yoga instructor herself, had told me, "I think someone should concentrate on your diagnosis and focus on your breathing situation. One-on-one is the best place for you to start. Go see Carmen."

My friend was correct. I had difficulty holding the tree pose for two seconds, so I asked Carmen if I could begin with the daisy pose. Her engaging smile diminished by a small degree, so I acquiesced, toning down my humor a tad until she got to know me better.

A yogi is anyone who practices yoga. I suppose that's true, but I was like Yogi the bear, especially attempting the low crescent moon pose (or was that the high crescent?).

After seven private sessions, I progressed to a restorative class. *This will restore your soul, Ann.* I tried to convince myself of that as I took the three-minute walk from my house to the first class. Each class was helpful, and I was relaxing more and breathing slower. My Mayo docs would be proud.

Would they put a star by my name on the poster, as I had given students back in my teaching days?

After a few months, I bumped it up a notch to a moderate class with another instructor, delightful Judy. Breathing deeply and relaxing consistently became the name of my game. Although the word *relaxed* had never fit in a description of me, that was about to change, and I would be the better for it.

I think I can. I think I can.

God has created our bodies to be intricately wonderful, until they get messed up, I pondered as I sauntered to class one day.

I was beginning to connect better with my breath and with my God. It was evident that my heavenly Daddy was using my functional breathing disorder to draw me closer to Him. How could I complain about that?

I read the class flyer: "The emphasis is on strength, mobility, flexibility, and various breathing techniques." The doctors at Mayo would be pleased with this new endeavor in the more challenging yoga group. Will I get another star? I wondered that as I wandered out after class that day.

"Breathe," Judy would say often. I needed her cue as a nudge. This was another way to retrain my brain as it reminded my body that I could breathe correctly. "It's our nature to hold our breath," she would repeat, with great patience. I needed to hear that often.

One day, the God of my heart gave me an acronym, a heartfelt acronym for the word *yoga*:

Y You,

O oh

G God,

A are awesome.

I decided that each time I was in the prayer pose during class, I would reverently repeat to myself, with a smile, "You, oh God, are awesome."

Some days, I would topple over when Judy introduced a new pose. Then God would remind me that I was a work in progress. He is so like that, I remembered, as I attempted to gain my balance once again. Having God as my cheerleader and best friend, assisting me in balancing everything in my life, was a blessing.

I kept on keepin' on. To me, yoga was just another vehicle, encouraging me to stop, relax, and breathe in His breath. A friend told me that yoga was merely technology to strengthen the body, mind, and spirit. I agree.

One day, I got brave enough to say to Judy, "I'm really sore at you. Or maybe I'm just really sore."

That was when I got into a plank and couldn't get from there to a downward-facing dog. I was a work in progress. Perhaps that was short for "in another five years, I might be adequate."

Yoga filled me with His peace and slowed me down, so I could hear Him better and then heed Him quicker. I sensed God saying, "Take care of yourself, Ann, so that I can use you to care for others." I understood that before I could bear burdens for others, I first had to bear my own.

Sometimes I wanted to sing out loud "Help," the tune by the Beatles, but decided a silent song was more fitting: *Help me get my feet back on the ground. Won't you please, please help me?* I quickly realized that singing to myself wasn't as effective.

As a response to my sister's poem at the beginning of this chapter, now my neck is not aching because of Him. My nerves are not breaking because of Him.

You,

oh

God,

are awesome.

After class one day, Judy said, "Ann, you look healthy." I absorbed that encouragement. She then complimented me on a pose I had done well and added, "You have perspective." We never know how a timely word will bolster up a discouraged soul. My shoulders were a little bit straighter and my gait lighter on my walk home.

It was apparent I was getting stronger each day, but there was no rest for the weary and no time to put my feet up and rejoice. Probably a 6 on the Richter scale of exhaustion, I now added needles to my breathing saga of fun. I actually counted one day; there were usually fifty of them during my acupuncture treatment. Mayo Clinic said that acupuncture would be beneficial to help correct my breathing, so I held my breath and jumped in, feet first.

I had heard that acupuncture restores the body, aids healing, and reduces stress. "I'll take all three," I said to Clark, who was busy getting the needles all lined up so didn't reply.

With the needles properly positioned in a variety of spots over my body and a heat lamp applied to a specific area of greatest need, Clark informed me that he would return in about fifteen minutes. I closed my eyes and prayed for stamina on this journey.

I once heard the analogy that when a garden hose is blocked, it cannot give water to the plant. That seemed to be the principle of acupuncture. By placing the needles in certain areas that seemed blocked, the water of breathing could water my body. God was using many avenues to work His plan to heal me, and acupuncture assisted me in learning to breathe correctly.

Have you ever tried acupuncture? Well, don't be afraid. After all, what harm can fifty needles do?

Or a yoga class.

One day, after Judy reminded us, for the umpteenth time, not to hold our breath but to focus on breathing, I sensed God revealing to me that I had held my breath through tough times in my life, to my own demise. Ouch.

The truth can hurt, but it can also heal, so I did some silent self-talk: "Ann, don't hold your breath, and remember to breathe in His breath." I had to remember to breathe, and sometimes I forgot.

But one thing was simple to recall:

You, ... oh ... God, ... are ... awesome.

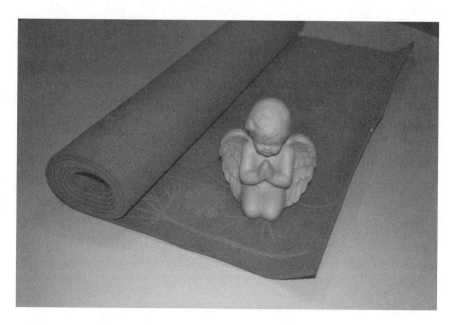

God Chair Journal Entry

Sovereign Lord,
Only by looking back can I see how far I've come.
What did You specifically mean when You said to "enjoy" soul-itude?

<u>E</u> Enjoy the
<u>N</u> "now" to be
<u>J</u> joyful
<u>O</u> over living in
<u>Y</u> Your world.

For example, Ann, taking slow walks and bubble baths, enjoying the deck and Pandora 1960s music, doing fun weekend activities, spending one long weekend out of town every month, living in the present.

Lord, help me to rest in my snail-like progress during Your healing of my breathing. I'll focus on enjoying Your world.
I'll stay in the day.
I promise.

And when you stumble, Ann, don't focus on those missteps. Just keep your eyes on Me.
Always.

CHAPTER 43

Shazam

"I have a giant of a God, you see, bigger than the trouble in front of me."
—Lowell Alexander, Larry Bryant, "Giant of a God"

When I was younger, Gomer Pyle made *Shazam* a household word. My now older life changed when God intervened through my Mayo doctors.

"You need to find a counselor who specializes in cognitive behavioral therapy," the staff at Mayo said. "That will retrain your brain to be able to breathe correctly. But go to several counselors to see who you best click with."

Several. *Hmmm.*

I knew I wanted a woman. There was no question that I wanted a godly woman. And this godly woman has to specialize in CBT. Where do I begin? *Shazam!* What a challenge. The balls were bouncing once again, and I had another difficult decision to make.

Where should I turn? Of course, I prayed first and then searched the internet. Sometimes I felt as if I were shooting in the dark yet was confident that God was guiding me.

Eventually, I located four counselors, making appointments with each. I had rapport with them all.

What do I do? They were all helping me with my breathing challenge, in a variety of ways.

I couldn't narrow them down to one, so I went to all four. One hour every week. For eternity, it seemed.

I purchased a notebook for each counselor. Why? Well, first, I'm a note-taker. Then there was homework from each one. And did I mention sessions with all four every week?

Life became more complicated by the day. Do I have the essentials for today's counselor? Yes, I did. Grabbing my purse, the correct notebook, and my ever-present blue pen, I headed out the door. Getting into my car, I felt in peril. Peril? Why did I hear that word?

Before starting the car, I looked up *peril*. "Serious and immediate danger." Well, I'm not in danger because each counselor is helping me.

But sessions with four? Every week? Homework for four? Every week? Along with physical therapy, three times every week? Then acupuncture and deep tissue massage once a month? And yoga twice a week.

I may not be in peril, but it surely feels that way today. *Shazam, I'm tired.*

I didn't know how to narrow the counselors down. They were becoming friends, and each one cared. I appreciated their sincere desire to assist me in this process toward complete healing. How could I decide?

After several months, filled with keeping the appointments straight, doing the homework, faithfully meditating on my assignments, and praying for wisdom, I settled on one counselor, which came as a relief.

"There's a brick in the right side of your brain," DeAnn said. My ears perked up as I was picturing the inside of my head. "You have to break the brick into tiny particles, sending those bits to the frontal lobe of your brain. Then the trauma you experienced won't have control over you anymore."

Shazam. I understood that, and it made sense.

"Let's forge ahead," I said to her, still not quite certain of the outcome but ready to go forward with vigor.

"Ann, your homework is to select one scripture to hang onto and a secular quote to go with it." More homework. I was ready to roll up my sleeves for a lengthy Bible search.

But God gave me the verse immediately. *Whew.* Philippians 1:6 was the one: "Being confident of this, that He who began a good work [in Ann] will carry it on to completion until the day of Christ Jesus" (NIV).

I was confident in God. After all, He had begun a good work in me, and completion was His goal for me.

For each of us.

Shazam. That was an easy verse to select.

Now for the secular quote. I had thought that would require more effort, but God sent it to me rather quickly. He knew I was weary. I don't even know who Robert Collier is, yet the quote meant a lot to my progress. Thank you, sir.

> Visualize this thing you want.
> See it, feel it, believe in it.
> Make your mental blueprint and begin.
> —Robert Collier

I wrote Philippians 1:6 and good ole Robert's quote on small cards and placed them at strategic places on the dashboard of my car. Neither took long to memorize, as I was always traveling from appointment to appointment. It's fun when God allows you to see His work coming to fruition. *Shazam*, He is good.

In the counseling sessions, I learned that what I think affects how I feel, which affects my actions. Think. Feel. Act.

Wondering if there might be a test, I committed those three words to memory. Then there was more to write in my notebook and learn. My brain responds to my mind. The brain wants to hop onto the distress cycle and remain there. Since my trauma experience, my body has been in control of my brain. My brain needs to be in control of my body, once more.

I came up with some coping songs to sing in the car and throughout my daily activities. One was to the tune of "Trust and Obey," which I knew well:

> Rest and relax.
> Just rest and relax.
> To be happy and breathing,
> just rest and relax.

Shazam. It was working. God knew that I was musical, so He provided me soothing songs and timely tunes.

To "If You're Happy and You Know It," He gave me:

> If you're happy and you know it
> Then your breath will surely show it.
> If you're happy and you know it, breathe deeply.

My counselor encouraged me to delve into reflective thoughts. Now, along with CBT, I would add trauma resolution therapy (TRT), a cleansing process.

"Ann, how have you been forced to change because of that medical event?" DeAnn explained to me that these were my survival responses, which became my homework.

After dealing with those issues over several weeks, I studied the secondary losses because of having to keep on going, to survive. Survival is all-encompassing, I reflected.

What had I lost because of the event? A great deal, I was to learn. This took much thought to uncover. I found that when God reveals, we can heal.

DeAnn showed me how to confront and grieve those losses. In this process, I was smashing the trauma brick in the right side of my brain. Then I would slowly move those tiny bits of pain to the front of my brain. Frontal lobe meant freedom, and I could almost envision the small particles slowly relocating to a healthy healing place. Ahh …

"Ann, as you are grieving the event and all that you lost because of it, you are regaining more power and control. Your homework is to celebrate your progress. What has God shown you? Reflect on that. Rejoice in it. Focus on your growth.

Another week, she ended our time together with, "God has been good to you. Your homework is to locate a scripture on healing, meditating on the ways that you are relying on God for complete restoration."

Taking all my homework assignments seriously, as any firstborn would, I brought back many verses to show her. Perhaps I thought I could get extra credit. It wasn't difficult to choose this one as my favorite, and I proudly read it to her:

Lord, Your discipline is good, for it leads to life and health. You have restored my health and have allowed me to live. (Isaiah 38:16 NLT)

"Today we will work on grounding tools, Ann." Another new term, I thought, as DeAnn continued talking while I continued taking notes. She explained each tool in depth and informed me that my homework was to choose three of the grounding tools and practice them.

- ice in hand
- word drop
- I spy
- muscles tense and relaxing
- mindfulness

Learning more with each session, I thought I might receive my own professional counseling license any day now.

I had heard that it's always darkest before the dawn, and I guess that's true. Although I was relying on God for the healing, I still had to do the hard work. Perhaps one day, I would arrive into the blessed light of day and complete health.

"Ann, let the open wound bleed." Wow. What a word picture. The bleeding allows the hurt to escape in order for me to heal. Then let the blood flow.

I began to daydream about her comment, but my attention came back to the surface of my mind quickly. "Now let's discuss a breathing process that will stimulate your vagus nerve. You will practice exhaling longer than you inhale. It's part of retraining your brain to be in control of your body, specifically the lungs."

Vagus nerve? CBT? TRT?

"All you are learning is empowering you, Ann." DeAnn encouraged me with her smile, probably because she noticed my furrowed brow. I'm such an open book.

I laughed so that I wouldn't cry. If I could cry.

When I handed God my health issues, He grabbed my hands and wouldn't let go. Little did I know that in our connection, He would create a gem of great beauty.

I remembered a song and added my own ending:

> I have a giant of a God with me.
> He is bigger than the trouble behind me,
> right in front of me, or yet to be seen.

Shazam.
He is good, indeed.

God Chair Journal Entry

Sovereign Lord,
The ivy is still connected to the tree but is now very brown. It can no longer hurt, cripple, damage, or kill that tall, green tree.

Ann, that's just like the trauma work in your counseling. The brick, hammered to smithereens, can move from the right side of the brain to the front, to no longer have power over you.

The ivy is still on the tree, but it can no longer hurt the tree, because now it has no power over it, right, Lord?

Ann, remember in the last storm when a large branch from that same tree was sliced away? That is what I had to do with you. There was a large branch in you, looking healthy, but causing you great pain, though you had pushed the pain deep down. I had to remove it.

Lord, without Your breath in my lungs, I can't breathe. Without Your breath in my heart, I can't live.

I allowed a breathing storm in your life in order to chop that branch off. There is still a weeping wound, like on the tree. You realized that a bandage wouldn't fix it. I am your Tree Surgeon. Watch Me work so that your heart can see how much I love you.

I am captivated by You, my Lord.

THE TRIUMPH

CHAPTER 44

Out of the Blue

The beginning of anxiety is the end of faith, and the
beginning of true faith is the end of anxiety.
—George Mueller

Out of the blue. That's how it came. My first normal breathing in nearly three years. God allowed it to occur two months into my treatment plan, when He knew that my throat was dry and my soul was parched.

I dreaded waking up each morning because opening my eyes meant just another day of misery. Then it happened. Unbeknownst to me, God was on the verge of sending another gift from His throne of grace. As I woke up, somewhere between actual sleep and slight dozing and full wakefulness, I felt it. Can it be? Out of the blue, I realized that I was breathing. Normally. I was never a stomach-sleeper but noticed that I was on my stomach, my head turned to the left on the pillow. What is this all about?

Do not move, Ann. This wonderful feeling of true breath might go away. Stay still. Remain calm. See what will happen. Those were my initial thoughts.

Soaking up the joy of this experience, I relaxed even more. Was that a slight smile of hope I sensed? It lasted about fifteen minutes; then, as quickly as it arrived, it vanished.

Where did it go? Why did it leave? I had felt the sensation of heaven for fifteen minutes. Before my very eyes. In my very bed.

But as quickly as the disappointment came, it left too. I smiled again, which surprised me. I felt like I was on a cloud, calmly floating. What a gift I received this morning from the God of the universe and the Master of my breath.

Lord, thank You. What a marvelous fifteen-minute break in my nonbreathing action. I'm so grateful. You love me so much. Then I realized exactly what He was doing and told Him so. I drew in as deep of a breath as possible and began:

You gave me a taste of the 100 percent healing that's awaiting me up ahead. Soon, perhaps? Maybe later? Sooner or later, it really doesn't matter, because all I feel in this moment is immense gratitude. To You. For this gift. It is a foretaste of the future that is controlled by You, and I will wait patiently.

I could face another difficult day with a spring in my step. He knew that I needed encouragement, and He had sent His breath, straight as an arrow, right into my heart, as well as to my brain. At that moment, bliss entered my anxious soul.

On another occasion, God arrived on the scene with a second out-of-the-blue present to me. This time, we were by the ocean, quite a few hours' drive from our home. My sunglasses, wide-brimmed hat, and book were in hand as I sat in the beach chair, poised to watch the water lapping onto the shore.

Then came a jolt from the excited grandchildren: "Dolphins, G.G. Look at the dolphins. They are over there. Can you see them?"

We were spending some time on Tybee Island, off the Georgia coast, making memories. Were the grandchildren seeing things they hoped to see, or did they really see a dolphin in the water? Squinting my eyes, I walked closer to the edge of the ocean, for I had never seen one in the wild myself. Chuckling about all the counseling terms I had learned, I wondered, could it be real and true?

My eyes bulged. "Yes! I do see them. Several."

For the next fifteen minutes, we watched God place dolphin after dolphin in front of us as another unexpected, but oh-so-appreciated, gift. Just because He could and because He loved us so. We all witnessed a spectacular spectacle.

It was only a couple of weeks later that a third out-of-the-blue experience came my way. I was packing to visit Mary Katherine, Patrick, and our grandchildren. My earthly protector didn't want me to go, but

I told Al, "I'm anxious about going to Chattanooga as well, but it's only for two days. It will be a good test of how my breathing is improving, or if it's not."

During my health issue, he had seen me come home so exhausted from making that nearly three-hour trip. I felt loved that he cared so much, yet I wanted to go, for them and for me. The two days in the Tennessee mountains flew by quickly. We made memories, yet again.

With my items in hand, I was heading back home. Holding my suitcase in one hand, I mentioned to Mary Katherine that I had a tad more energy on this trip, making my fingers look like what I thought a tad meant. I felt encouraged. *Al will be glad to hear that report when I return,* I thought, standing a little taller with pride.

Then, out of the blue and out of my mouth, the words flew without warning: "And God is going to heal me 100 percent by my birthday." Seriously?

What did I just say? My eyes got large. Shocked, I placed my hand over my mouth for several seconds, which seemed like hours. Life seemed to be in slow motion. I didn't know what had happened or why it had happened, but I was amazed, to say the least. What was God up to?

"I didn't mean to say that," I breathlessly told her. "Those weren't my words." Then whose were they?

I chose to believe that God was giving me a sneak peek into His time frame for healing me. I'm going to hang on to this gift that's coming. It's up ahead, and I know that for sure. Fake it till you make it, Ann.

It was a more pleasant drive back home. Was the car floating on a cloud, or was I the one floating? It was hard to tell. In the car, talking alone with God, I whispered, "What a God sighting. Al will be so excited to hear this news."

Not too long after that out-of-the-blue happening, while having lunch with a friend, I bragged on God about those words that had escaped from my mouth, unannounced.

Without so much as a pause, Candi leaned over the table and exclaimed with glee, "Ann, you prophesied over yourself."

I did what? My knowledge of prophesying was sparse, but Candi had the gift of prophesy and recognized it right away. God was letting me know, through her, that what I had said was truth. His truth. To a heart that was weary with the wait. He was letting me know there would be an end. He lovingly revealed it to me in front of our daughter.

Returning home, I turned on my comfy-feeling old movie channel. We had become best buds. Expecting to find a 1940s drama, instead I was viewing the last ten minutes of *I Walked with a Zombie*.

What? No, I confidently claimed. *I walk with God. And sometimes, He comes to me out of the blue to keep me encouraged, and it keeps me going.*

That evening, the God-conversation continued as I relaxed in bed. *Lord, I yearn to pass each test along this health trek with excellence. You are my Pilot. I'm enjoying the flight, most of the time. I'm all in, Sir.*

Better than dolphin sightings are God sightings, I decided calmly. *Lord, I appreciate the privilege to be in the middle of watching You work. What a blast of wonder and joy.*

As my eyes moved back to the television screen, I wondered, *Should I watch the last few minutes of* I Walked with a Zombie? In a split-second, I turned on another *Andy Griffith* episode. A wiser choice, for sure.

I didn't ask for this pain. So why did I get it? Ann was here one day and gone the next. What is the deal here?

It was all becoming clear. To my eyes and my heart. The deal was that God was doing His job. It had little to do with my breathing and more to do with my spiritual growth. Game changer.

You are overwhelmingly patient with Little Annie Rooney, Lord. And as Daddy says often, "You are great in Your goodness and good in Your greatness."

Was that another God sighting? I was beginning to learn that sightings from Him can be spotted around every corner if I have eyes to see and ears to hear.

It was Lois Evans who said, "If God showed us the whole journey, we'd never take the first step."

A country song, by Ronnie Milsap, filtered through my mind with a slight lyric change, so I sang to Him:

"I wouldn't have missed it for the world" (the breathing issue, that is, Lord).

God Chair Journal Entry

Sovereign Lord,
Thank You for being who I need, and in being who I need, You are what I need. When You are who and what I need, You are all that I need, and I depend on You for every breath.

Lord, the sky is so blue, no clouds to be seen. Why did You decide that the sky would be blue (and not red, green, or purple)?

Ann, I made the sky blue so that people would want to turn their eyes toward heaven and be soothed by the color I chose, resting and relaxing in the soothing calmness of the color blue. So look up at Me and be calmed. Remember, I created human beings, so be calm and enjoy the world I have provided.

I enjoyed being with You in my God chair, Lord.

Me too, Ann. Let's keep it up.

CHAPTER 45

Manna for Each Moment

Then the Lord said to Moses [and Ann], I will rain down
bread from heaven for you. The people are to go out each
day and gather enough for that day. In this way I will test
them and see whether they will follow my instructions.
—Exodus 16:4 (NIV)

"**W**hat is it?" That's what the word *manna* means. God allowed me to be
sick for thirty-three months. One thousand days is a long, long, long time.
Try it, if you dare.

Sometimes it seemed more like a deathwatch. Was I already dead or
just slowly dying? I didn't want to be His Recalcitrant Ann, but on more
days than I cared to mention, I was just that. In His goodness, God still
came to me repeatedly, to remind me of what I knew to be real and true:

"Ann, you are My wonderful creation. Rest in the knowledge that what
I'm allowing is all for your good and My glory." I needed those reminders
daily.

God was gracious. Each day, He provided manna as my moment-by-
moment provision. On days when I wasn't at my best, I resented valuable
time I thought I was losing along the three-year journey. *Is this the trip
to nowhere, Lord?* I waited and watched. Then the manna started falling.

Manna through His Word.

Manna through His people.

Manna through Himself.

I wasn't losing but gaining. Do I sometimes appear to be an Israelite?

Happy and then not? The scales were removed from my eyes, and everything became clear. I could be secure in each day's provision because it was always enough.

In the morning, He offered my heart grace and mercy for the needs of that day. No more. No less.

The next day, I awoke to more awaiting manna. It smelled so good to my soul. Fresh-baked. Warm. Made by the hands of the One who loved me the most. How could my heart resist? He was the Best Manna Baker around.

I looked forward to the light of a new day, keeping my eyes peeled for each manna message. He never failed. There was manna for that day, then the day that was tomorrow, then the day that was next week, then the day that became a journey of a thousand days.

God was reminding me that manna for the day is always enough. He revealed His provision to me, one day at a time. *Sir, as I'm depending on the manna, I am learning to depend on You more with each passing day.*

It's amazing what humans will do to survive. I was in survival mode for forever, it seemed, desperate to make it through another twenty-four hours. I often wondered if I could continue or even had the desire to go on.

"Ann, you became desperate for me. That was on my to-do list, as I have been teaching you that dependence on Me is far better than independence, which you hear from the world's teachers. You know Matthew 6:34 well. Here is where the rubber meets the road, so put it into practice. 'Therefore [Ann] do not worry about tomorrow, for tomorrow will worry about itself. Each day has enough trouble of its own'" (NLT).

Some manna came to my anxious heart by people who became "Jesus with skin on." Over the three years, which seemed like three hundred years, precious people sent caring cards. These are a few lines of lingering love in my manna menagerie:

- "May you feel that beautiful peace of mind that comes from knowing He hears all your prayers."
- "You are in my prayers. You are not well, but this will pass."
- "His healing power is already at work in you."
- "Now is the time to rest, to pray, and to accept the love and nurturing of others. This is often hard to do."

- "I am still praying that you are making lots of progress as you move along through the healing process."
- "You are a special lady, and I'm praying for answers regarding your health."
- "So sorry to hear of your trial. Praying that it will be resolved very soon."
- "You couldn't be in better hands than His."
- "I keep you in my prayers. Hope you're feeling better soon, like yesterday."
- "Accepting love can be as important as giving, so please remember that I am praying for you."
- "I know the day will soon come when you are feeling whole again and grateful for the gift of wellness."
- "Sending lots of smiles your way and praying for peace from Jesus and good results at Mayo."
- "Here's a long-distance hug."

Helen Keller coined a great truth: "Walking with a friend in the dark is better than walking alone in the light." And she would know.

I humbly thanked my Lord for "friend manna." The words they spoke walked with me through the dark days.

Other marvelous manna along the jumbled journey came in the form of

- morning coffee and prayer, delivered to my bed by Al,
- encouraging texts and emails,
- Sunday sermons, meant just for me,
- Christian radio, alone in my car with Him,
- cards from family, friends, and soon-to-be friends,
- caring staff at Choices Pregnancy Care Center,
- time prostrate before the Lord in the local prayer tower,
- Marvelous Mayo (need I say more?),
- psalms, hymns, and spiritual songs (Ephesians 5:19),
- praying when I couldn't sleep,
- staying "in the day," enjoying Him,
- the comfort of new friends,

- silently singing when I had no voice,
- learning to cry better,
- people praying throughout the country,
- realizing how fragile life is,
- the blessing of no missed opportunities,
- allowing others the privilege of being my burden bearers,
- redeeming the time for a hurting world who needs Him,
- intentionally blooming where He plants me,
- listening to Him, with no agenda,
- relishing every moment in my God chair, and
- learning to be.

Lord, every morning You gave me what-is-it. Each day, Your what-is-it for me was varied because You knew the pain in my heart. You provided just the right what-is-it, sustaining me during the seemingly never-ending walk. I'm grateful, Sir. I'm better for it, which was Your plan all along. Gratitude. Being humbly grateful seems so small but so huge in spiritual growth. When I miss the moments, I miss moments with You.

Thank You for loving me enough to grind me to a halt for the short term so that I could grow closer to You and more effectively serve You for the long term. Your miraculous manna for each moment was Your gift to me.

C. S. Lewis phrased it well: "Either we say Jesus Christ is a great man, or we fall on our faces and say, 'He is Lord.'"

You are, indeed, my Lord, for one thousand days and until I meet You face to face, laying my crown at Your feet in adoration.

Manna messages made manna memories.

God Chair Journal Entry

Sovereign Lord,
You give me amazing gifts, and I am in awe of Your awesomeness.

Ann, I know what it will take to draw people into a deeper relationship with Me. For you, in this time and place, it was a medical procedure that went awry.

Lord, I read that the definition of awry is "away from the appropriate, planned, or expected course; with a turn or a twist to one side; crooked, distorted, out of place; the situation is falling apart, unraveling, chaotic, disorderly; not the expected outcome."

Ann, in the physical realm, the above is true. In the heavenly realm, My plan for you, when the medical issue occurred, wasn't falling apart or unraveling or chaotic or disorderly. My expected outcome for you was all for your good because I am a good God.

Lord, I was hurt so that I could be helped so that I could be healed, all for Your glory and for my good. You are, indeed, my amazing God.

I am filled with gratitude for Your providential care.

CHAPTER 46

Healed by the Healer

Then he said to me, "Prophesy to these bones and say
to them, 'Dry bones, hear the word of the Lord! This is
what the Sovereign Lord says to these bones: I will make
breath enter you, and you [Ann] will come to life.'"
—Ezekiel 37:4, 5 (NIV)

A child's eyes sparkle with anticipation when given a gift. My sparkling surprise came to fruition on June 6, 2018. What an exciting, long-awaited gift it was. Just four months prior, I had prophesied over myself while at our daughter's house that God would heal me 100 percent by my birthday. At the time, I was hopeful but not convinced.

My improvement came in baby steps. Al said that I was breathing deeper at night. The physical therapist made positive comments, as did the acupuncturist. Then the massage therapist chimed in, as she commented on my improvement. I bragged to the yoga instructor about the deeper breathing I noticed. Getting up the nerve, I whispered to my counselor, "It makes me feel nervous to say it, but I think that I'm 80 percent healed."

She smiled, nodding in agreement with my assessment.

The Sunday before my Wednesday birthday, while riding to church, I worked up my courage again.

"Al, God has healed me," I said in a soft voice yet with calm boldness.

He was like a deer in the headlights, almost running into a ditch. "Really?" he responded, shocked.

During the worship service, I heard in my spirit, "Thirty-three months."

What does thirty-three months mean? I asked God and myself.

I sensed Him revealing "thirty-three months to the day."

Are you trying to tell me something, Lord?

Then I saw it so clearly. The procedure that had triggered the functional breathing disorder occurred on August 6, 2015. My upcoming birthday was to be June 6, 2018, a few days from now.

Counting the months on a piece of paper where I would be taking sermon notes in a few minutes, I realized that I had just completed a thirty-three-month classroom journey with God.

But wait. I also had my first Mayo Clinic appointment on December 6, 2017. Curiosity was getting the best of me. Did the number 6 mean something, and what was the significance of the number 33, if any?

So many times along my rocky health path, I had forcefully called out to God. I knew that He was holding my hand, yet I became weary in the waiting.

I looked in my daily devotional book as soon as we arrived back home. A year ago, the Bible verse for the devotional that day read:

Until now you have not asked for anything in My name. Ask and you will receive, and your joy will be complete. (John 16:24 NIV)

I had written in the margin:

"Dear God, who loves me deeply, and in the powerful name of Jesus, I ask You to heal my breathing problem."

Healing comes from the hands of God. God mended me, physically, emotionally, mentally, and spiritually. He doesn't just concern Himself with one area of our lives. He loves us totally: body, mind, soul, and spirit.

The deceiver stole my breath for a season. His plan was to destroy me. He lost. I won.

When God gave me a "breathe-through" in my life in June 2018, it became a "breakthrough" in my walk with Him.

1 Corinthians 3:6 (NIV) reminds us, "I planted the seed, Apollos watered it, but God has been making it grow."

To that, I say, "Mayo Clinic made the diagnosis, Ann worked their treatment plan, but God gave the healing."

Healed by the Healer, indeed.

Barbara Johnson wrote, "Prayer is asking for rain, and faith is carrying the umbrella." Need I say more?

God had allowed my life to worsen in order to show what a Dynamic Deliverer He is.

I prayed, carried the umbrella, and breathed a sigh of relief.

God Chair Journal Entry

Sovereign Lord,
I see a glimmer of sun. It has been so rainy lately. The sun is so soothing.
Thank You for being the Soother of my soul.

Ann,
If the Son sets you free, You are free indeed.

Lord,
I receive Your freedom to breathe.
I receive the gift of breathing.
I receive the gift of relaxed breathing.
I receive the gift of 100 percent breathing.
I receive the gift of peaceful breathing.
I receive the gift of constant breathing.
I receive Your breath in me.
I believe Your breath is a part of me.
I believe Your words to me are true.
I believe.

I'm so very grateful to You for healing my breathing and growing me closer
to You.

My pleasure, Ann. And although I don't work for Chick-Fil-A, the people
they employ are some of My instruments in this hurting world too.

CHAPTER 47

What's in a Number?

Teach us to number our days, that we [Ann]
may gain a heart of wisdom.
—Psalm 90:12 (NIV)

August 6, 2015   •   the medical event
December 6, 2017   •   first day at Mayo Clinic
June 6, 2018   •   birthday and healing day

My functional breathing disorder dissipated by my sixty-seventh birthday, just as God had graciously revealed to me four months earlier. The prophesy had come to fruition. The Great Physician had healed me.

Each significant event had the number 6 in it. What does the number 6 mean in the Bible? Upon research, I learned that the number 6 is significant because it illustrates the imperfection in man's work. It is a human number. The number 6 is related to men and women and their imperfections or shortcomings.[3]

The number 6 not only signifies labor but also sorrow. There is no rest unless we have peace with God. I had prayed that concerning others. "God, give them no rest and no peace until they find their rest and peace in You." Praying that so often, I had memorized it. That same prayer was for me too.

My breathing issue was here "for a spell," as my grandparents used to say. At the time, I had no idea just how long a spell would be. Maybe that was a good thing.

Before my health challenge, I wouldn't have given you two hoots and a holler for a breath. Breathing was nothing I thought I should express gratitude for. But after breathing became a commodity, I would gladly give you two hoots and a holler, plus five screams along the way, if it would help.

God, You are my panacea, my cure-all, the solution and remedy for all difficulties and diseases. You are my heavenly elixir, my godly wonder drug.

Part of Exodus 15:26 reads "for I am the Lord that healeth thee" (KJV).

Lord, You do solve all my problems and cure all my diseases, physically, emotionally, mentally, and spiritually. What a mandated epiphany.

A. W. Tozer stated it well: "The reason why many are still troubled, still seeking, still making little forward progress is because they haven't come to the end of themselves. We're still trying to give orders and interfering with God's work within us."

Lord, I've learned that Your healing in my life is not like flipping a light switch. It takes time because You are teaching me volumes of lessons along the way. This path of healing has been a joyful journey with You.

So what about thirty-three months, the total duration of my illness? It turns out that the number 33 connects to a promise or the promises of God.[4] He had promised me healing but also had promised to walk alongside me up to the top of the healing mountain.

For each of those long months, I called on God in a deeper way as never before. He answered me, speaking to my heart, showing me things that only a lengthy tough time can teach.

The words "my flesh" appear thirty-three times in the King James Bible.[5] My flesh cried out daily for more relief and more of Him. I trusted. He provided. I rejoiced.

And the word "separated" is in God's Word thirty-three times in the King James Bible.[6] God lovingly allowed me isolation from others, separated from normal activities, in order to transform me, making me brand new.

Our spine contains thirty-three bones, holding our body straight.[7] God effortlessly held me erect, strong, and straight as He maneuvered my life and channeled my heart as I moved into a deeper walk with Him.

And what about one thousand days encompassing those thirty-three months? Biblically, I learned that the number 1,000 symbolizes immensity, a fullness of quantity, or multitude.[8]

On August 6, 2015, when the medical event occurred, I had no idea of the daunting task ahead.

During the prolonged process, I was filled to the brim, first with confusion, then frustration, and finally filled to the utmost with all of Him, not just more of Him.

I learned a multitude of life lessons along the way. God can teach us much in one thousand days. Actually, He can teach us much in just one day, if our ears are open and our hearts are receptive.

Over the years, I would tell people that I wasn't a numbers girl, which was why I married a banker with a master's in business administration. After all, if He had wanted me to do math, He wouldn't have made it so hard.

So what's in a number? It turned out that numbers meant a great deal to God and to my listening ear. He spoke so clearly to my heart that numbers connected the dots to His work in me during my healing process.

"For a day in Your courts [and in my God chair] is better than a thousand elsewhere" (Psalm 84:10a ESV).

It turns out that I am a numbers girl, after all. Please tell Al.

God Chair Journal Entry

Sovereign Lord,
I am sitting in a different spot on the deck, so as I look up, I have a different perspective.

Ann, that is true of your life too. During your many days of functional breathing disorder, your perspective at first was on getting well. Then, as I led you into the wonderful wilderness, your focus became enjoying the experience and learning of Me.

May I never be satisfied with my old life and the status quo, Sir.

Ann, now you are getting it. One of the many purposes for the thousand-day journey was so that you would never be satisfied with anything that is not all of Me. Your perspective on life has changed forever.

Lord, when I want a way out of a situation, I find a way in, into Your throne room by way of my God chair. That's where I allow You to make a way where there seems to be no way.

Thanks be to God.

Yes, Ann. Thanks be to Me.

CHAPTER 48

A Front-Row Seat

I will sing to the Lord as long as I live. I will
praise my God to my last breath.
—Psalm 104:33 (NLT)

When the long saga ended and my healing came to fruition, a variety of people asked, "Didn't you feel like Job some days?" No, I didn't. Really. Frustrated? Often. Job-like? Never. I kept asking God to teach me what He knew I needed to learn during the challenging three years.

However, I do identify with a section of James 5:11 (ESV) that reads, "Behold, we consider those blessed who remained steadfast. You have heard of the steadfastness of Job, and you have seen the purpose of the Lord, how the Lord is compassionate and merciful." God gave me courage through the trial; for He knew the outcome: that a new and improved Ann would emerge from her cocoon, transformed forever.

A pastor once told me that the Hebrew root of "be still" in Psalm 46:10 means "let go." I have also heard that "stop striving" is accurate too.

Stop striving and let go, Ann; know that God is God.

Stop striving and let go, Ann; know that God is.

Stop striving and let go, Ann; know.

Stop striving and let go, Ann.

Stop striving, Ann.

Stop.

Much to my chagrin, I had lived most of my 67 years thinking, planning, and mentally living a next-thing-to-do mindset while physically existing in the now. How sad. But no more. The thing at hand would be the thing *in* hand. I committed to reside, remain, and rejoice in the Bible verse that tomorrow would take care of itself.

I am learning to stop more. And listen. God stopped me in my tracks on August 6, 2015, until I cried, "Uncle" … or did I cry, "Lord"?

Alistair Begg said, "If I spend my last breath proclaiming Jesus, all will be well."

Here are a few things He taught me along the way:

- Great things can come from great adversity.
- God is more concerned with healing my soul than healing my health.
- Living in the old me is not where I choose to remain.
- Growing pains are painful because they are supposed to be painful.
- Pain sends me to the foot of the cross to find help in time of need.
- The Lord loves me, despite me.
- The glory is in the struggle.
- My Creator knows what I need.
- The Captain of my soul loves me too much to leave me where I am.
- Life is tough, but God is tougher.
- Being made holy surpasses being made happy.
- Surprises from God, though difficult, can become delights.
- In my discomfort, I find His comfort.

God doesn't waste our pain. It has a purpose, both inside us and outside to the world.

I can breathe. How incredible is that? All things being equal, those horrendous days of pain wouldn't have been my first choice for learning truths from Him. But in hindsight, God knew exactly what I needed, and He became my Reliant Rock. I marvel at the mountain He took me over. Profusely and on bended knee, I begged Him to let me walk an easier route, just like the Israelites wanted. But He knew best.

Hope and despondency were at my disposal daily, each vying for the prize. On a good day, I decisively chose hope. Another day, despondency won the scary skirmish. But deep down in my soul, I was confident that He had already won the war, so I allowed Him to light my pathway.

Two months before my healing, I read 2 Samuel 5:20, noticing that Baal-perazim means "the Lord bursts through." I wrote in the margin of my Bible, "He will burst through my breathing issue."

And on my birthday, June 6, 2018, I read in a devotional book, "Every good and perfect gift is from above, coming down from the Father of the heavenly lights, who does not change like shifting shadows" (James 1:17 NIV). Underneath my birthdate, I added, "100 percent healed." I have heard the phrase "trust your gut,' but I say, "Trust your God."

God's purpose for me is to grow. And to grow, I have to be with Him. And when I'm with Him, I can do more for Him.

For three years, God gave me a front-row seat in watching Him do His best work in my battered being. I'm not much above five feet tall and always appreciate the front seat of anything: in a car, at a play or sports event.

Wintley Phipps made a potent statement on pain of any kind when he said, "It is in the quiet crucible of your personal private suffering that your noblest dreams are born and God's greatest gifts are given in compensation for what you've been through."

So the moral to my story is, don't take His presence or His presents, some of which don't seem like good gifts for a season, for granted. Whatever draws you and me closer to God is worth the pain and the price.

Breathe in this new day, and may God's breath be your joy and sustenance, as it has become mine. He is not finished with you if He has given you breath for today.

And He might just be saving you a front-row seat to watch Him at work.

God Chair Journal Entry

Sovereign Lord,

This morning, the sound of the cars and machines doing work outside distracted me. I'd rather hear the birds and You, always.

Ann, sometimes in life, you have to hear the positive things, or you will drown in the negative things. Block out the noise, and you will be able to hear the birds and Me.

I'll choose delight over distractions, Lord. The longer I walk with You, the more I have to share with others. My three years were a paradox. Painful moments but bountiful growth.

Lord, I am thankful to You for

- ears to hear,
- breath to breathe,
- "refirement" to slow down,
- time to listen to You,
- learning that You shoulder the world's issues so I don't have to,
- hearing the wind of the Holy Spirit,
- enjoying a balanced marriage,
- knowing You love our two children and grandchildren more than I can,
- being able to trust You,
- all You've taught me in a thousand days,
- the hard times that have stretched me,
- TMJ that reminds me to rest in Your sovereignty, and
- all You are teaching me each day in my God chair.

Ann, your thirty-three heavenly healing months are in the past, but the lessons you learned remain in your heart forever. I prepared you, equipped you, and molded you as a burden bearer. That is your calling. It was a thousand-day preparation in your wonderful wilderness, wasn't

it? Now you can allow the river of life to flow out of you to a hurting world. Go with Me, Ann.

Thank You, Lord, for removing life's distractions through my health issue so that I could focus on You. You used three years of shallow breathing as the platform to do great things in me.

Ann, I created birth and death, as well as the dash in between. Be intentional about what you put in the dash of your existence.

Lord, here I go ... June 6, 1951–????
<u>D</u> Daring to
<u>A</u> ask my
<u>S</u> Savior
<u>H</u> how to spend each moment.

CHAPTER 49

To Be or Not To Be; That Is the Question

Where can I go and meet with God?
—Psalm 42:2b (NIV)

Sovereign Lord,
How great Thou art.

I like snuggles with my man, my children, and my grandchildren. Snuggles with my God are even better, and I get the best God snuggles alone with You in my God chair. I am blessed.

"Ann, you bless Me by taking the time to be in My presence. I watch how My truth takes root in the soil of your soul each time you sit attentively at my feet. You are my little girl."

Lord, being in my God chair is heavenly liberation. I enjoy our dynamic dialogues and yearn for a deeper kind of listening. Each day, I look forward to lingering with You, and listening to You, and learning from You. Or sometimes just being quiet beside You, covered by a fuzzy shawl when it's chilly, viewing the comforting Amazing Grace cross on the floor by the hearth, with the notepad and pen on the floor a short distance away, and putting my soft peace slippers on my always cold feet.

"Ann, I noticed that you used the word *being* twice in that paragraph. You are progressing in just being, aren't you? Being with Me and being with yourself. You are growing, and that puts a smile on My countenance."

Lord, Your smile lights my day, for You are my shield and my shelter. I excelled at doing for too many years to count. Now I'm also good at being. It sounds so very simple, but it takes daily effort. What a privilege to be calm in order to hear Your still, small voice that is oh, so comforting and powerful. What a relief to feel the freedom to rest, relax, and restore. And I can have those three Rs just by being in Your presence. Why didn't I learn that sooner?

"Ann, your times are in My hands. Chill out, forget the past, and keep learning of Me. I am thrilled when you choose to be with Me."

Lord, in my God chair, I learned that when I am silent before You, You are not silent with me. The more often I sit with You, the more I hear from You.

Sometimes I chuckle when I reflect on the fact that You gave me no peace until I agreed to write this book about You and Your work in me to change me into a better Ann. By just being and sitting alone in Your presence, but not lonely. Sitting with You, just us two, and yet having an audience of One. What patience You possess, Lord. Thank You for being patient with me on this journey we call life. It's an honor to soak up my Savior.

"Ann, people jokingly say that someone 'has the patience of Job.' No one has more patience and bountiful mercy, as well as amazing grace, than I do. Keep tapping into My resource every day. That act will continue to grow you closer to Me each day until I take You home."

Lord, You showed me that the God chair isn't usually prayer; it's being there in Your presence, with no agenda getting in our way. You, the God of the universe, listening to each question. And I, being quiet to hear the unequaled voice of Your answer. You continually teach me to be patient with myself in the process of waiting for You to respond.

"There's that *patient* word again, Ann. You are learning patience from the Master of Patience. That quality will be useful in your relationships with people I place in your path. Just keep leaning on Me."

Lord, I get it now. You love. I receive Your love. Then I send out Your love to others. You allowed my breath to be shallow for a season while you replaced it with a deeper relationship with You.

God, through His providence, had grown me spiritually as He had healed me physically. It was wonderful to have both self-care and God-care as I was sitting in my God chair. I felt such permeating peace. I knew that this was another God moment.

A few momentous minutes went by. Yet another opportunity to practice patience. I broke through the solemn silence with the Lord of my life and whispered, "I'm curious, Sir."

He didn't rush my next thoughtful sentence. The wait was long, but I could feel that He didn't mind the lingering time. Probably because time meant nothing to Him. And shouldn't to me. He knew that the wait positioned me for a purpose and that the purpose was always for His glory and my good. I quietly cleared my throat and timidly continued our dialogue.

Lord, will anyone else start a God chair?

He said nothing at first. I had learned that sometimes there is holy silence for holy reasons. I waited, having been on the path of patience from spending time with Him, knowing that He would respond if I were quiet, still, and willing to allow time to meander along when I was in His precious presence.

I sat, gazing at the fluffy clouds that He was floating by just for me to enjoy. I was being with Him, in the moment, learning how to wait well.

Then, out of the blue, but right on cue, I sensed Him peering deeply into the eyes of my soul, the way only He can gaze. I knew that this was to be another God sighting, and I was eager to receive His word to my waiting heart.

"You have asked Me an inquisitive question of 'Will anyone else start a God chair?' So here is my answer. It's actually very simple, yet also most complex.

"To be or not to be, Ann; that is always the question."

Profound words from the Father of wonderful words.

I sensed that our time was over for the day. I had been in the presence of the King of kings. He yearned to spend all the time in the world with me. Just us two. I must be very special to Him.

Getting up from the wing-backed chair with ease and a spring in my step, I placed my peace slippers under the chair, positioned the shawl in its home on the back arm, stretched a bit, pushed my shoulders back, looked up to heaven, and smiled.

He smiled back.

Then, I breathed.

The actual God chair with throw blanket, Amazing
Grace cross on hearth, peace slippers, with the God
journal and blue pen a distance away.

"NOTHING ELSE"

Cody Carnes
Songwriters: Hank Bentley, Cody Carnes, Jessie Early

I'm caught up in Your presence.
I just want to sit here at Your feet.
I'm caught up in this holy moment.
I never want to leave.

Oh, I'm not here for blessings
Jesus, You don't owe me anything
More than anything that You can do
I just want You.

If we cooperate with Him in loving obedience, God will manifest Himself
to us, and that manifestation will be the difference between a nominal
Christian life and a life radiant with the light of His face.

—A. W. Tozer

IT'S REAL AND IT'S TRUE: GOD LOVES YOU

It is my custom on each birthday to ask the Lord for a motto for the upcoming birthday year. He gave this one to me on June 6th, 2018:

> I'm sixty-seven, and I know I'm going to heaven.
> Do you?

There is no greater question for you to consider in order to be confident and certain that you are heaven bound. But mere knowledge and information are not enough.

If you know that a ticket and a passport are required to board an airplane, yet you arrive at the gate without either, you won't fly anywhere.

If you are at the beach and know that the lifeguard is prepared to rescue people, but you are happily sitting on your towel on the sand, that lifeguard is not saving you. If an undertow takes you out, you will beg with all your might for the lifeguard to rescue you.

Have you believed, received, and taken hold of Jesus as your passport as well as your lifeguard to save you, taking you safely to heaven? If not, He's only information.

I'm sixty-seven, and I know I'm going to heaven. Do you?

S Suddenly

A aware of

C Christ's

R royalty,

I in

F faith, as

I I journey

C closer to

E eternity with Him.

He sacrificed His life for me.
I now sacrifice my life for Him.
I am nothing. He is everything.

(Debra Folsom contributed the airplane and lifeguard illustrations.)

AFTERWORD

"Refirement" was the term I gave for my retirement. My theory was that if I'm doing nothing for the Lord and His Kingdom each day, He might as well take me to my eternal home now. Therefore, I'm refired for whatever He has in store for me until I am called home or hear the trumpet sound.

Little did I know that during the first part of my refirement, I would be plunged into the fire of adversity. I wouldn't have chosen one thousand days of hard health issues followed by a lengthy recovery.

God continued, in His kind and loving way, to reassure me that this was merely a bump in the road, a time of preparation. After all, He had called me as a burden bearer, and I was confident that He was chiseling my rough edges to get me ready.

He is not yet finished with changing me for the better. Nor has He completed His work in you. After all, we're still breathing, aren't we?

I appreciate being able to breathe better than most people do, probably. You may be grateful for other healings: cancer, prodigal child, devastating divorce; the list could go on. Have I not listed yours? Then do so on this line:_____

Are you wearily waiting for your healing and wondering if it will ever arrive? Has it lasted more than a million days? If so, I can't imagine your pain.

What I can offer, in your tough time, is a song that ministered to me, both during my long illness and after God allowed me to breathe again. Listen to the lyrics and rest in Him, assured that He will use even us. "Let Me Sing," by songwriter Andrew Peterson, speaks more profoundly than I ever could. This is the powerful chorus:

> So let me sing for the love.
> Let me love for the lost.

> Let me lose all I have
> for what I found on the cross.
> Let me trust You with my life.
> Let me live to give You praise.

Be blessed along your journey with Him, and I'll see you in heaven.

Who knew that my illness would be His book to a hurting world? Only God.

Soli Deo Gloria (Glory to God alone).

Sydney Ann Beckham Gainey
(aka Little Annie Rooney)

And a postscript from Corrie ten Boom to you and to me:

> I know that the experiences of our lives, when we let
> God use them, become the mysterious and perfect
> preparation for the work He will give us to do.

WANT MORE?

Email me at breatheinhim2@gmail.com. It will bless me as I read what our Mighty God is teaching you.

If you have set up your own God chair, tell me all about that too. Let me know what it looks like.

After you complete the "For Personal Pondering" section, I'd like to hear some of your insights.

Check out my website, both to contact me about speaking engagements or to order a book for a friend or for a small group study. I have spoken to groups from California to Michigan to South Carolina and all parts in between and would be honored to visit your corner of the world. My website is www.annbgaineyauthor.com.

Elizabeth Searle Lamb must have a God chair, for she speaks precisely of what I've experienced:

"Now do I go apart from the world? I close the outer door that I may not be distracted by people. I sit comfortably relaxed, still and serene."

"Now I close the door of my mind on the outer things. Peace, peace, I say. I rest now, quietly, without word, without thought, without emotion. Peace, be still."

"Now I center my attention, my concern, on God. I look to God, peacefully relaxed, serene, and quiet."

"Slowly I begin to feel that inner stillness grow and encircle me. A sort of spiritual sunlight envelops me. I am warm and comforted. I am quiet with a living quietness. Here in this holy communion with God, I am re-created. I am healed. I am blessed in all ways. And I am shown the work God would have me do."

"I am enveloped in the spiritual sunshine of divine love, both loving and receiving love within that radiant glow. And I give thanks. Amen."

FOR PERSONAL PONDERING

Chapter 1

Be honest with God about your thoughts when you feel out of your comfort zone.

Meditate on the lyrics of "To the Table" (songwriters: Jonathon Smith, Zach Williams, Tony Wood).

Chapter 2

Share with your Maker a time when you were whirling out of control and thank Him for calming you down.

Listen to the song "Something Good" (songwriters: Mark Harris, Anthony Skinner, Kyle Lee).

Chapter 3

If you are a crier, thank Him. If you aren't, ask Him for healing tears. He desires to pour them into you and down your cheeks.

Hear Him speak in "Hold Me While I Cry" (songwriter: Gerald Crabb).

Chapter 4

Say, "Hold me, Jesus," when you wake up in the night.

Think about His love for you in the song "Hold Me, Jesus" (songwriter: Richard Mullin).

Chapter 5

Talk to God about a time when you felt that He just might be hibernating.

Listen to "Savior's Shadow" (songwriters: Blake Shelton, Jessi Alexander, Jon Randall).

Chapter 6

Consider a way to say "thank you" to someone who has been Jesus with skin on for you.

Ponder that thought through the song "Even If" (songwriters: Bart Millard, Ben Glover, Crystal Lewis, David Garcia, Tim Timmons).

Chapter 7

When have you questioned a hard blessing?

Try listening to "Blessings" (songwriter: Laura Story).

Chapter 8

Talk with God about a "stinging time" you have experienced.

The "Eye of the Storm" might help you with the stings (songwriter: Ryan Stevenson).

Chapter 9

When did God lovingly refine you through trials, temptations, and tests?

"It is Well with My Soul" will be sung at my funeral (songwriters: Horatio Spafford and Philip Bliss).

Chapter 10

Reflect on a time when you didn't think that what was occurring could possibly be for your good.

Remember that He does hold it all together by reading the lyrics of "You Hold It All Together" (songwriters: Leslie Jordan, David Leonard, Sandra McCracken).

Chapter 11

How did you feel when you were suffering and everyone else appeared happy?

Perhaps the song "Even Then" will minister to your heart (songwriters: Kyle Lee, Micah Tyler, Tony Wood).

Chapter 12

Think of a time when you couldn't do what had once given you joy. How did that feel?

The lyrics of "Life Song" may be of comfort (songwriter: John Mark Hall).

Chapter 13

Maybe TMJ isn't your Achilles' heel. Go to God with whatever is chronically painful for you.

Ponder the old gospel song "Little David" (sung by The Freemans).

Chapter 14

When have you felt emotionally frozen?

Listen to "Into Dust" and chronicle your feelings to Him (songwriter: Mac Brock).

Chapter 15

How has not knowing something made life difficult for you?

This song ministers to my heart. Perhaps yours, too: "The Lord Is My Salvation" (songwriters: Keith and Kristyn Getty).

Chapter 16

Think of a time when you had to make a tough decision.

Our God is truly the "Center of It All" (songwriters: Brent Milligan, Heather Joel, Phil Joel).

Chapter 17

What hard place has God sent you, and what did He teach you along the rough road?

The lyrics of "I Will Follow" may touch you (songwriters: Bryan Fowler, Dan Bremnes).

Chapter 18

When were you excited and anxious at the same time?

Listen to "Move" and be encouraged on your journey (songwriters: Bryan Fowler, Toby McKeenan, Christopher Stevens).

Chapter 19

Talk with your Good Shepherd about a tough time and how it drew you right into His arms.

Listen to "I'd Rather Go through Something with Him" (songwriters: Donald Wallace Poythress, Kenna Turner West, Karen Gaye Peck).

Chapter 20

Has your Protector given you great favor? Thank Him.

In fact, "Praise Him" (songwriter: Shane Barnard).

Chapter 21

When were you relieved to know that you were fighting to stand strong in the strength of His might?

The lyrics of "Pass through the Waters" are soothing (songwriter: Dan Burgess).

Chapter 22

The turquoise cross was a gift from God to me. What has the Giver of every perfect gift provided for you?

What's it like to know that "My Feet Are on the Rock" (songwriters: Abbie Parker, Josh Bronleewe, Lindsey Sweat, Matthew Hein)?

Chapter 23

Has time seemed cold to your very existence?

Sing, with confidence, "Your Grace Is Enough" (songwriter: Matt Maher).

Chapter 24

When did your evening turn to morning?

Lord, thank You that "You Never Walk Away" (songwriter: London Gatch).

Chapter 25

Have you had a diagnosis that was tough to hear?

Then, "Just Be Held" in His arms (songwriters: Mark Hall, Matthew West, Bernie Herms).

Chapter 26

For what have you prayed and watched Him supply?

These lyrics will remind you to rejoice when you hear the "Sound of Surviving" (songwriters: Nichole Nordeman, Tommee Profitt).

Chapter 27

What happened when you were a deer in the headlights?

"As the Deer" will put yourself in the deer's place (songwriter: Martin J. Nystrom).

Chapter 28

Thank God for how He pulled you out from under the awful avalanche.

Rejoice that His love for you is "Wide, High, Long, Deep" (songwriters: Ellie Holcomb, Nathan Dugger).

Chapter 29

People are a blessing, but God is the best.

Tell Him "There Is No One Like You" (songwriters: Andy Harrison, Joth Hunt, Sam Evans).

Chapter 30

What Mayo experience has God given to you? God will heal your heart if you allow Him.

Listen to "Heal" and be open to the healing (songwriter: Tom Peter Odell).

Chapter 31

When were you relieved to get home to safety?

Meditate on "Hope in Front of Me" (songwriters: Brett James, Danny Gokey, Bernie Herms).

Chapter 32

Did you have to "work a plan" with God supervising?

He is faithful to "Do It Again" in every tough time (songwriters: Mack Brock, Chris Brown, Matt Redman, Stephen Furtick).

Chapter 33

Share with God how you felt when you preferred warm heat or cooling ice, but He didn't give it to you.

Soothe your heart with the words of "Storehouse" (sung by the Grey Havens; songwriters: Dave Radford and Licia Radford).

Chapter 34

Thank the Lover of your soul for moving unhealthy muscles and unyielding mountains for you.

Listen to "Tell Your Heart to Beat Again" (songwriters: Bernie Herms, Randy Phillips, Matthew West).

Chapter 35

List the times that God has been patient with you, and ask Him for opportunities for your patience to flourish.

To do this, you have to "Be Still and Know" (songwriter: Steven Curtis Chapman).

Chapter 36

Think about the pressure to do rather than to be.

It lessens the pressure if you "Breathe" (songwriters: Jonny Diaz, Jonathan Smith, Tony Wood).

Chapter 37

Can you accept the Restful Redeemer's permission to rest?

Say to Him, "Jesus, I Am Resting, Resting" (songwriters: David Hampton, Jean Sophia Pigott).

Chapter 38

Did you view your last wilderness as a wonderful time?

In all this, we say, "Blessed Be Your Name" (songwriters: Beth Redman, Matt Redman).

Chapter 39

Tell God that you yearn to be in the trenches with Him.

It is easier if I "Fix My Eyes" on Him at all times (songwriters: Seth Mosley, Joel Smallbone, Joel David Smallbone, Luke Smallbone).

Chapter 40

What smells draw you closer to the Lord of your life? Lavender, perhaps?

I'm glad that He is "Unfinished" with you and me (songwriters: Ben Glover, Colby Wedgeworth).

Chapter 41

Reflect with God on your "real but not true" experiences.

I serve the One who will "Hold Me Together." You do too (songwriters: Chuck Butler, Tauren Wells, Tony Wood).

Chapter 42

Say aloud, "You, oh God, are awesome," and give Him specifics.

I'm safe when I can "Just Be Held" by my Lord (songwriters: Mark Hall, Bernie Herms, Matthew West).

Chapter 43

Think of a shazam moment and thank Him for it.

Say out loud, "There Is No One like You" (songwriters: Sam Evans, Andy Harrison, Joth Hunt).

Chapter 44

Thank God for when He came to you "out of the blue."

Hooray for "Your Great Love" (sung by Covenant Worship).

Chapter 45

How has he blessed you with manna when you were starving for manna messages?

Listen to the lyrics of "They Will Be Filled" (songwriters: Thomas Williamson, Scott Willis).

Chapter 46

In what physical, emotional, mental, and spiritual areas of life have you been healed by the Healer?

Rejoice that He makes "All Things New" (songwriters: Mack Brock, Chris Brown, Wade Joye, Ben Richter).

Chapter 47

Research numbers that may have significance for you.

Surely, you can "Count That High" (songwriters: Jordan Feliz, Ross King, Jordan Sapp).

Chapter 48

When did your Mighty Master provide you with a front-row seat to watch Him work?

The song "Available to You" will reveal your gratitude (songwriter: Scott Willis).

Chapter 49

Converse with God about the challenge to just be, admitting your hesitancy to start your own God chair.

The song "Just Want You" may help you begin the talk (songwriter: Travis Greene).

It's Real and It's True

After you ask Him into your heart, say, "I Want to Thank You, Lord" (songwriter: Scott Willis).

Then you can "Come to the Table" (songwriters: Dave Frey, Ben Glover, Ben McDonald).

Afterword

This is a meaningful "Benediction" (songwriter: Scott Willis).

Now it's "Only Jesus" in your life (songwriters: Mark Hall, Bernie Herms, Matthew West).

More

Aren't you glad we have a "Living Hope" (songwriters: Brian Mark Johnson, Phil Wickham)?

NOTES

Chapter 14

1   Pigott, Jean Sophia. "Jesus, I Am Resting, Resting."

Chapter 27

2   "Firefighter Saves Deer Stranded on Slippery Ice." YouTube, December 12, 2017. *Washington Post.*

Chapter 47

3   "Numerology in Bible or Biblical Numerology Numbers." November 12, 2010. AstroVera.com.
4   "The Number 33." YouTube. January 26, 2017. God's Perfect Word.
5   Ibid.
6   Ibid.
7   Ibid.
8   "The Meaning of Numbers: The Number 1000." December 8, 2015. scripturerevealed.com.

ABOUT THE AUTHOR

Being in church every time the doors opened was Ann's norm, the firstborn growing up in the home of a pastor, his wife, a brother, a sister, a dog and an occasional parakeet and turtle. She taught in public and Christian schools after receiving a Bachelor of Arts in Education from Erskine College and a Master of Education from Clemson University. Ann re-fired, her word for retired, after serving for 25 years as the executive director of Choices Pregnancy Care Center in Gainesville, Georgia, where God grew her spiritually by leaps and bounds. She learned how to be "Jesus with skin on" to hurting people. Al and Ann have two adult children, two grandchildren and are knocking on the door of celebrating their 50th wedding anniversary, by God's grace.